C-1082   CAREER EXAMINATION SERIES

This is your
PASSBOOK for...

Administrative Trainee

Test Preparation Study Guide
Questions & Answers

COPYRIGHT NOTICE

This book is SOLELY intended for, is sold ONLY to, and its use is RESTRICTED to individual, bona fide applicants or candidates who qualify by virtue of having seriously filed applications for appropriate license, certificate, professional and/or promotional advancement, higher school matriculation, scholarship, or other legitimate requirements of education and/or governmental authorities.

This book is NOT intended for use, class instruction, tutoring, training, duplication, copying, reprinting, excerption, or adaptation, etc., by:

1) Other publishers
2) Proprietors and/or Instructors of "Coaching" and/or Preparatory Courses
3) Personnel and/or Training Divisions of commercial, industrial, and governmental organizations
4) Schools, colleges, or universities and/or their departments and staffs, including teachers and other personnel
5) Testing Agencies or Bureaus
6) Study groups which seek by the purchase of a single volume to copy and/or duplicate and/or adapt this material for use by the group as a whole without having purchased individual volumes for each of the members of the group
7) Et al.

Such persons would be in violation of appropriate Federal and State statutes.

PROVISION OF LICENSING AGREEMENTS – Recognized educational, commercial, industrial, and governmental institutions and organizations, and others legitimately engaged in educational pursuits, including training, testing, and measurement activities, may address request for a licensing agreement to the copyright owners, who will determine whether, and under what conditions, including fees and charges, the materials in this book may be used them. In other words, a licensing facility exists for the legitimate use of the material in this book on other than an individual basis. However, it is asseverated and affirmed here that the material in this book CANNOT be used without the receipt of the express permission of such a licensing agreement from the Publishers. Inquiries re licensing should be addressed to the company, attention rights and permissions department.

All rights reserved, including the right of reproduction in whole or in part, in any form or by any means, electronic or mechanical, including photocopying, recording, or by any information storage and retrieval system, without permission in writing from the Publisher.

Copyright © 2024 by
National Learning Corporation

212 Michael Drive, Syosset, NY 11791
(516) 921-8888 • www.passbooks.com
E-mail: info@passbooks.com

PUBLISHED IN THE UNITED STATES OF AMERICA

PASSBOOK® SERIES

THE *PASSBOOK® SERIES* has been created to prepare applicants and candidates for the ultimate academic battlefield – the examination room.

At some time in our lives, each and every one of us may be required to take an examination – for validation, matriculation, admission, qualification, registration, certification, or licensure.

Based on the assumption that every applicant or candidate has met the basic formal educational standards, has taken the required number of courses, and read the necessary texts, the *PASSBOOK® SERIES* furnishes the one special preparation which may assure passing with confidence, instead of failing with insecurity. Examination questions – together with answers – are furnished as the basic vehicle for study so that the mysteries of the examination and its compounding difficulties may be eliminated or diminished by a sure method.

This book is meant to help you pass your examination provided that you qualify and are serious in your objective.

The entire field is reviewed through the huge store of content information which is succinctly presented through a provocative and challenging approach – the question-and-answer method.

A climate of success is established by furnishing the correct answers at the end of each test.

You soon learn to recognize types of questions, forms of questions, and patterns of questioning. You may even begin to anticipate expected outcomes.

You perceive that many questions are repeated or adapted so that you can gain acute insights, which may enable you to score many sure points.

You learn how to confront new questions, or types of questions, and to attack them confidently and work out the correct answers.

You note objectives and emphases, and recognize pitfalls and dangers, so that you may make positive educational adjustments.

Moreover, you are kept fully informed in relation to new concepts, methods, practices, and directions in the field.

You discover that you are actually taking the examination all the time: you are preparing for the examination by "taking" an examination, not by reading extraneous and/or supererogatory textbooks.

In short, this PASSBOOK®, used directedly, should be an important factor in helping you to pass your test.

ADMINISTRATIVE TRAINEE

DUTIES
Performs beginning level staff work in the process of learning varied and special administrative assignments. Performs related duties as required.

SCOPE OF THE EXAMINATION
The <u>written test</u> will cover knowledge, skills and/or abilities in such areas as:

1. Arithmetic reasoning;
2. Evaluating conclusions in light of known facts;
3. Preparing written material;
4. Understanding and interpreting tabular material; and
5. Understanding and interpreting written material.

HOW TO TAKE A TEST

I. YOU MUST PASS AN EXAMINATION

A. WHAT EVERY CANDIDATE SHOULD KNOW

Examination applicants often ask us for help in preparing for the written test. What can I study in advance? What kinds of questions will be asked? How will the test be given? How will the papers be graded?

As an applicant for a civil service examination, you may be wondering about some of these things. Our purpose here is to suggest effective methods of advance study and to describe civil service examinations.

Your chances for success on this examination can be increased if you know how to prepare. Those "pre-examination jitters" can be reduced if you know what to expect. You can even experience an adventure in good citizenship if you know why civil service exams are given.

B. WHY ARE CIVIL SERVICE EXAMINATIONS GIVEN?

Civil service examinations are important to you in two ways. As a citizen, you want public jobs filled by employees who know how to do their work. As a job seeker, you want a fair chance to compete for that job on an equal footing with other candidates. The best-known means of accomplishing this two-fold goal is the competitive examination.

Exams are widely publicized throughout the nation. They may be administered for jobs in federal, state, city, municipal, town or village governments or agencies.

Any citizen may apply, with some limitations, such as the age or residence of applicants. Your experience and education may be reviewed to see whether you meet the requirements for the particular examination. When these requirements exist, they are reasonable and applied consistently to all applicants. Thus, a competitive examination may cause you some uneasiness now, but it is your privilege and safeguard.

C. HOW ARE CIVIL SERVICE EXAMS DEVELOPED?

Examinations are carefully written by trained technicians who are specialists in the field known as "psychological measurement," in consultation with recognized authorities in the field of work that the test will cover. These experts recommend the subject matter areas or skills to be tested; only those knowledges or skills important to your success on the job are included. The most reliable books and source materials available are used as references. Together, the experts and technicians judge the difficulty level of the questions.

Test technicians know how to phrase questions so that the problem is clearly stated. Their ethics do not permit "trick" or "catch" questions. Questions may have been tried out on sample groups, or subjected to statistical analysis, to determine their usefulness.

Written tests are often used in combination with performance tests, ratings of training and experience, and oral interviews. All of these measures combine to form the best-known means of finding the right person for the right job.

II. HOW TO PASS THE WRITTEN TEST

A. NATURE OF THE EXAMINATION

To prepare intelligently for civil service examinations, you should know how they differ from school examinations you have taken. In school you were assigned certain definite pages to read or subjects to cover. The examination questions were quite detailed and usually emphasized memory. Civil service exams, on the other hand, try to discover your present ability to perform the duties of a position, plus your potentiality to learn these duties. In other words, a civil service exam attempts to predict how successful you will be. Questions cover such a broad area that they cannot be as minute and detailed as school exam questions.

In the public service similar kinds of work, or positions, are grouped together in one "class." This process is known as *position-classification*. All the positions in a class are paid according to the salary range for that class. One class title covers all of these positions, and they are all tested by the same examination.

B. FOUR BASIC STEPS

1) Study the announcement

How, then, can you know what subjects to study? Our best answer is: "Learn as much as possible about the class of positions for which you've applied." The exam will test the knowledge, skills and abilities needed to do the work.

Your most valuable source of information about the position you want is the official exam announcement. This announcement lists the training and experience qualifications. Check these standards and apply only if you come reasonably close to meeting them.

The brief description of the position in the examination announcement offers some clues to the subjects which will be tested. Think about the job itself. Review the duties in your mind. Can you perform them, or are there some in which you are rusty? Fill in the blank spots in your preparation.

Many jurisdictions preview the written test in the exam announcement by including a section called "Knowledge and Abilities Required," "Scope of the Examination," or some similar heading. Here you will find out specifically what fields will be tested.

2) Review your own background

Once you learn in general what the position is all about, and what you need to know to do the work, ask yourself which subjects you already know fairly well and which need improvement. You may wonder whether to concentrate on improving your strong areas or on building some background in your fields of weakness. When the announcement has specified "some knowledge" or "considerable knowledge," or has used adjectives like "beginning principles of…" or "advanced … methods," you can get a clue as to the number and difficulty of questions to be asked in any given field. More questions, and hence broader coverage, would be included for those subjects which are more important in the work. Now weigh your strengths and weaknesses against the job requirements and prepare accordingly.

3) Determine the level of the position

Another way to tell how intensively you should prepare is to understand the level of the job for which you are applying. Is it the entering level? In other words, is this the position in which beginners in a field of work are hired? Or is it an intermediate or advanced level? Sometimes this is indicated by such words as "Junior" or "Senior" in the class title. Other jurisdictions use Roman numerals to designate the level – Clerk I, Clerk II, for example. The word "Supervisor" sometimes appears in the title. If the level is not indicated by the title, check the description of duties. Will you be working under very close supervision, or will you have responsibility for independent decisions in this work?

4) Choose appropriate study materials

Now that you know the subjects to be examined and the relative amount of each subject to be covered, you can choose suitable study materials. For beginning level jobs, or even advanced ones, if you have a pronounced weakness in some aspect of your training, read a modern, standard textbook in that field. Be sure it is up to date and has general coverage. Such books are normally available at your library, and the librarian will be glad to help you locate one. For entry-level positions, questions of appropriate difficulty are chosen – neither highly advanced questions, nor those too simple. Such questions require careful thought but not advanced training.

If the position for which you are applying is technical or advanced, you will read more advanced, specialized material. If you are already familiar with the basic principles of your field, elementary textbooks would waste your time. Concentrate on advanced textbooks and technical periodicals. Think through the concepts and review difficult problems in your field.

These are all general sources. You can get more ideas on your own initiative, following these leads. For example, training manuals and publications of the government agency which employs workers in your field can be useful, particularly for technical and professional positions. A letter or visit to the government department involved may result in more specific study suggestions, and certainly will provide you with a more definite idea of the exact nature of the position you are seeking.

III. KINDS OF TESTS

Tests are used for purposes other than measuring knowledge and ability to perform specified duties. For some positions, it is equally important to test ability to make adjustments to new situations or to profit from training. In others, basic mental abilities not dependent on information are essential. Questions which test these things may not appear as pertinent to the duties of the position as those which test for knowledge and information. Yet they are often highly important parts of a fair examination. For very general questions, it is almost impossible to help you direct your study efforts. What we can do is to point out some of the more common of these general abilities needed in public service positions and describe some typical questions.

1) General information

Broad, general information has been found useful for predicting job success in some kinds of work. This is tested in a variety of ways, from vocabulary lists to questions about current events. Basic background in some field of work, such as sociology or economics, may be sampled in a group of questions. Often these are principles which have become familiar to most persons through exposure rather than through formal training. It is difficult to advise you how to study for these questions; being alert to the world around you is our best suggestion.

2) Verbal ability

An example of an ability needed in many positions is verbal or language ability. Verbal ability is, in brief, the ability to use and understand words. Vocabulary and grammar tests are typical measures of this ability. Reading comprehension or paragraph interpretation questions are common in many kinds of civil service tests. You are given a paragraph of written material and asked to find its central meaning.

3) Numerical ability

Number skills can be tested by the familiar arithmetic problem, by checking paired lists of numbers to see which are alike and which are different, or by interpreting charts and graphs. In the latter test, a graph may be printed in the test booklet which you are asked to use as the basis for answering questions.

4) Observation

A popular test for law-enforcement positions is the observation test. A picture is shown to you for several minutes, then taken away. Questions about the picture test your ability to observe both details and larger elements.

5) Following directions

In many positions in the public service, the employee must be able to carry out written instructions dependably and accurately. You may be given a chart with several columns, each column listing a variety of information. The questions require you to carry out directions involving the information given in the chart.

6) Skills and aptitudes

Performance tests effectively measure some manual skills and aptitudes. When the skill is one in which you are trained, such as typing or shorthand, you can practice. These tests are often very much like those given in business school or high school courses. For many of the other skills and aptitudes, however, no short-time preparation can be made. Skills and abilities natural to you or that you have developed throughout your lifetime are being tested.

Many of the general questions just described provide all the data needed to answer the questions and ask you to use your reasoning ability to find the answers. Your best preparation for these tests, as well as for tests of facts and ideas, is to be at your physical and mental best. You, no doubt, have your own methods of getting into an exam-taking mood and keeping "in shape." The next section lists some ideas on this subject.

IV. KINDS OF QUESTIONS

Only rarely is the "essay" question, which you answer in narrative form, used in civil service tests. Civil service tests are usually of the short-answer type. Full instructions for answering these questions will be given to you at the examination. But in case this is your first experience with short-answer questions and separate answer sheets, here is what you need to know:

1) **Multiple-choice Questions**

Most popular of the short-answer questions is the "multiple choice" or "best answer" question. It can be used, for example, to test for factual knowledge, ability to solve problems or judgment in meeting situations found at work.

A multiple-choice question is normally one of three types—
- It can begin with an incomplete statement followed by several possible endings. You are to find the one ending which *best* completes the statement, although some of the others may not be entirely wrong.
- It can also be a complete statement in the form of a question which is answered by choosing one of the statements listed.

- It can be in the form of a problem – again you select the best answer.

Here is an example of a multiple-choice question with a discussion which should give you some clues as to the method for choosing the right answer:

When an employee has a complaint about his assignment, the action which will *best* help him overcome his difficulty is to
- A. discuss his difficulty with his coworkers
- B. take the problem to the head of the organization
- C. take the problem to the person who gave him the assignment
- D. say nothing to anyone about his complaint

In answering this question, you should study each of the choices to find which is best. Consider choice "A" – Certainly an employee may discuss his complaint with fellow employees, but no change or improvement can result, and the complaint remains unresolved. Choice "B" is a poor choice since the head of the organization probably does not know what assignment you have been given, and taking your problem to him is known as "going over the head" of the supervisor. The supervisor, or person who made the assignment, is the person who can clarify it or correct any injustice. Choice "C" is, therefore, correct. To say nothing, as in choice "D," is unwise. Supervisors have and interest in knowing the problems employees are facing, and the employee is seeking a solution to his problem.

2) True/False Questions

The "true/false" or "right/wrong" form of question is sometimes used. Here a complete statement is given. Your job is to decide whether the statement is right or wrong.

SAMPLE: A roaming cell-phone call to a nearby city costs less than a non-roaming call to a distant city.

This statement is wrong, or false, since roaming calls are more expensive.

This is not a complete list of all possible question forms, although most of the others are variations of these common types. You will always get complete directions for answering questions. Be sure you understand *how* to mark your answers – ask questions until you do.

V. RECORDING YOUR ANSWERS

Computer terminals are used more and more today for many different kinds of exams.

For an examination with very few applicants, you may be told to record your answers in the test booklet itself. Separate answer sheets are much more common. If this separate answer sheet is to be scored by machine – and this is often the case – it is highly important that you mark your answers correctly in order to get credit.

An electronic scoring machine is often used in civil service offices because of the speed with which papers can be scored. Machine-scored answer sheets must be marked with a pencil, which will be given to you. This pencil has a high graphite content which responds to the electronic scoring machine. As a matter of fact, stray dots may register as answers, so do not let your pencil rest on the answer sheet while you are pondering the correct answer. Also, if your pencil lead breaks or is otherwise defective, ask for another.

Since the answer sheet will be dropped in a slot in the scoring machine, be careful not to bend the corners or get the paper crumpled.

The answer sheet normally has five vertical columns of numbers, with 30 numbers to a column. These numbers correspond to the question numbers in your test booklet. After each number, going across the page are four or five pairs of dotted lines. These short dotted lines have small letters or numbers above them. The first two pairs may also have a "T" or "F" above the letters. This indicates that the first two pairs only are to be used if the questions are of the true-false type. If the questions are multiple choice, disregard the "T" and "F" and pay attention only to the small letters or numbers.

Answer your questions in the manner of the sample that follows:

32. The largest city in the United States is
    A. Washington, D.C.
    B. New York City
    C. Chicago
    D. Detroit
    E. San Francisco

1) Choose the answer you think is best. (New York City is the largest, so "B" is correct.)
2) Find the row of dotted lines numbered the same as the question you are answering. (Find row number 32)
3) Find the pair of dotted lines corresponding to the answer. (Find the pair of lines under the mark "B.")
4) Make a solid black mark between the dotted lines.

VI. BEFORE THE TEST

Common sense will help you find procedures to follow to get ready for an examination. Too many of us, however, overlook these sensible measures. Indeed, nervousness and fatigue have been found to be the most serious reasons why applicants fail to do their best on civil service tests. Here is a list of reminders:

- Begin your preparation early – Don't wait until the last minute to go scurrying around for books and materials or to find out what the position is all about.
- Prepare continuously – An hour a night for a week is better than an all-night cram session. This has been definitely established. What is more, a night a week for a month will return better dividends than crowding your study into a shorter period of time.
- Locate the place of the exam – You have been sent a notice telling you when and where to report for the examination. If the location is in a different town or otherwise unfamiliar to you, it would be well to inquire the best route and learn something about the building.
- Relax the night before the test – Allow your mind to rest. Do not study at all that night. Plan some mild recreation or diversion; then go to bed early and get a good night's sleep.
- Get up early enough to make a leisurely trip to the place for the test – This way unforeseen events, traffic snarls, unfamiliar buildings, etc. will not upset you.
- Dress comfortably – A written test is not a fashion show. You will be known by number and not by name, so wear something comfortable.

- Leave excess paraphernalia at home – Shopping bags and odd bundles will get in your way. You need bring only the items mentioned in the official notice you received; usually everything you need is provided. Do not bring reference books to the exam. They will only confuse those last minutes and be taken away from you when in the test room.
- Arrive somewhat ahead of time – If because of transportation schedules you must get there very early, bring a newspaper or magazine to take your mind off yourself while waiting.
- Locate the examination room – When you have found the proper room, you will be directed to the seat or part of the room where you will sit. Sometimes you are given a sheet of instructions to read while you are waiting. Do not fill out any forms until you are told to do so; just read them and be prepared.
- Relax and prepare to listen to the instructions
- If you have any physical problem that may keep you from doing your best, be sure to tell the test administrator. If you are sick or in poor health, you really cannot do your best on the exam. You can come back and take the test some other time.

VII. AT THE TEST

The day of the test is here and you have the test booklet in your hand. The temptation to get going is very strong. Caution! There is more to success than knowing the right answers. You must know how to identify your papers and understand variations in the type of short-answer question used in this particular examination. Follow these suggestions for maximum results from your efforts:

1) Cooperate with the monitor

The test administrator has a duty to create a situation in which you can be as much at ease as possible. He will give instructions, tell you when to begin, check to see that you are marking your answer sheet correctly, and so on. He is not there to guard you, although he will see that your competitors do not take unfair advantage. He wants to help you do your best.

2) Listen to all instructions

Don't jump the gun! Wait until you understand all directions. In most civil service tests you get more time than you need to answer the questions. So don't be in a hurry. Read each word of instructions until you clearly understand the meaning. Study the examples, listen to all announcements and follow directions. Ask questions if you do not understand what to do.

3) Identify your papers

Civil service exams are usually identified by number only. You will be assigned a number; you must not put your name on your test papers. Be sure to copy your number correctly. Since more than one exam may be given, copy your exact examination title.

4) Plan your time

Unless you are told that a test is a "speed" or "rate of work" test, speed itself is usually not important. Time enough to answer all the questions will be provided, but this does not mean that you have all day. An overall time limit has been set. Divide the total time (in minutes) by the number of questions to determine the approximate time you have for each question.

5) Do not linger over difficult questions

If you come across a difficult question, mark it with a paper clip (useful to have along) and come back to it when you have been through the booklet. One caution if you do this – be sure to skip a number on your answer sheet as well. Check often to be sure that you have not lost your place and that you are marking in the row numbered the same as the question you are answering.

6) Read the questions

Be sure you know what the question asks! Many capable people are unsuccessful because they failed to *read* the questions correctly.

7) Answer all questions

Unless you have been instructed that a penalty will be deducted for incorrect answers, it is better to guess than to omit a question.

8) Speed tests

It is often better NOT to guess on speed tests. It has been found that on timed tests people are tempted to spend the last few seconds before time is called in marking answers at random – without even reading them – in the hope of picking up a few extra points. To discourage this practice, the instructions may warn you that your score will be "corrected" for guessing. That is, a penalty will be applied. The incorrect answers will be deducted from the correct ones, or some other penalty formula will be used.

9) Review your answers

If you finish before time is called, go back to the questions you guessed or omitted to give them further thought. Review other answers if you have time.

10) Return your test materials

If you are ready to leave before others have finished or time is called, take ALL your materials to the monitor and leave quietly. Never take any test material with you. The monitor can discover whose papers are not complete, and taking a test booklet may be grounds for disqualification.

VIII. EXAMINATION TECHNIQUES

1) Read the general instructions carefully. These are usually printed on the first page of the exam booklet. As a rule, these instructions refer to the timing of the examination; the fact that you should not start work until the signal and must stop work at a signal, etc. If there are any *special* instructions, such as a choice of questions to be answered, make sure that you note this instruction carefully.

2) When you are ready to start work on the examination, that is as soon as the signal has been given, read the instructions to each question booklet, underline any key words or phrases, such as *least, best, outline, describe* and the like. In this way you will tend to answer as requested rather than discover on reviewing your paper that you *listed without describing*, that you selected the *worst* choice rather than the *best* choice, etc.

3) If the examination is of the objective or multiple-choice type – that is, each question will also give a series of possible answers: A, B, C or D, and you are called upon to select the best answer and write the letter next to that answer on your answer paper – it is advisable to start answering each question in turn. There may be anywhere from 50 to 100 such questions in the three or four hours allotted and you can see how much time would be taken if you read through all the questions before beginning to answer any. Furthermore, if you come across a question or group of questions which you know would be difficult to answer, it would undoubtedly affect your handling of all the other questions.

4) If the examination is of the essay type and contains but a few questions, it is a moot point as to whether you should read all the questions before starting to answer any one. Of course, if you are given a choice – say five out of seven and the like – then it is essential to read all the questions so you can eliminate the two that are most difficult. If, however, you are asked to answer all the questions, there may be danger in trying to answer the easiest one first because you may find that you will spend too much time on it. The best technique is to answer the first question, then proceed to the second, etc.

5) Time your answers. Before the exam begins, write down the time it started, then add the time allowed for the examination and write down the time it must be completed, then divide the time available somewhat as follows:
   - If 3-1/2 hours are allowed, that would be 210 minutes. If you have 80 objective-type questions, that would be an average of 2-1/2 minutes per question. Allow yourself no more than 2 minutes per question, or a total of 160 minutes, which will permit about 50 minutes to review.
   - If for the time allotment of 210 minutes there are 7 essay questions to answer, that would average about 30 minutes a question. Give yourself only 25 minutes per question so that you have about 35 minutes to review.

6) The most important instruction is to *read each question* and make sure you know what is wanted. The second most important instruction is to *time yourself properly* so that you answer every question. The third most important instruction is to *answer every question*. Guess if you have to but include something for each question. Remember that you will receive no credit for a blank and will probably receive some credit if you write something in answer to an essay question. If you guess a letter – say "B" for a multiple-choice question – you may have guessed right. If you leave a blank as an answer to a multiple-choice question, the examiners may respect your feelings but it will not add a point to your score. Some exams may penalize you for wrong answers, so in such cases *only*, you may not want to guess unless you have some basis for your answer.

7) Suggestions
   a. Objective-type questions
      1. Examine the question booklet for proper sequence of pages and questions
      2. Read all instructions carefully
      3. Skip any question which seems too difficult; return to it after all other questions have been answered
      4. Apportion your time properly; do not spend too much time on any single question or group of questions

5. Note and underline key words – *all, most, fewest, least, best, worst, same, opposite,* etc.
6. Pay particular attention to negatives
7. Note unusual option, e.g., unduly long, short, complex, different or similar in content to the body of the question
8. Observe the use of "hedging" words – *probably, may, most likely,* etc.
9. Make sure that your answer is put next to the same number as the question
10. Do not second-guess unless you have good reason to believe the second answer is definitely more correct
11. Cross out original answer if you decide another answer is more accurate; do not erase until you are ready to hand your paper in
12. Answer all questions; guess unless instructed otherwise
13. Leave time for review

   b. Essay questions
1. Read each question carefully
2. Determine exactly what is wanted. Underline key words or phrases.
3. Decide on outline or paragraph answer
4. Include many different points and elements unless asked to develop any one or two points or elements
5. Show impartiality by giving pros and cons unless directed to select one side only
6. Make and write down any assumptions you find necessary to answer the questions
7. Watch your English, grammar, punctuation and choice of words
8. Time your answers; don't crowd material

8) Answering the essay question

Most essay questions can be answered by framing the specific response around several key words or ideas. Here are a few such key words or ideas:

M's: manpower, materials, methods, money, management
P's: purpose, program, policy, plan, procedure, practice, problems, pitfalls, personnel, public relations

   a. Six basic steps in handling problems:
1. Preliminary plan and background development
2. Collect information, data and facts
3. Analyze and interpret information, data and facts
4. Analyze and develop solutions as well as make recommendations
5. Prepare report and sell recommendations
6. Install recommendations and follow up effectiveness

   b. Pitfalls to avoid
1. *Taking things for granted* – A statement of the situation does not necessarily imply that each of the elements is necessarily true; for example, a complaint may be invalid and biased so that all that can be taken for granted is that a complaint has been registered

2. *Considering only one side of a situation* – Wherever possible, indicate several alternatives and then point out the reasons you selected the best one
3. *Failing to indicate follow up* – Whenever your answer indicates action on your part, make certain that you will take proper follow-up action to see how successful your recommendations, procedures or actions turn out to be
4. *Taking too long in answering any single question* – Remember to time your answers properly

IX. AFTER THE TEST

Scoring procedures differ in detail among civil service jurisdictions although the general principles are the same. Whether the papers are hand-scored or graded by machine we have described, they are nearly always graded by number. That is, the person who marks the paper knows only the number – never the name – of the applicant. Not until all the papers have been graded will they be matched with names. If other tests, such as training and experience or oral interview ratings have been given, scores will be combined. Different parts of the examination usually have different weights. For example, the written test might count 60 percent of the final grade, and a rating of training and experience 40 percent. In many jurisdictions, veterans will have a certain number of points added to their grades.

After the final grade has been determined, the names are placed in grade order and an eligible list is established. There are various methods for resolving ties between those who get the same final grade – probably the most common is to place first the name of the person whose application was received first. Job offers are made from the eligible list in the order the names appear on it. You will be notified of your grade and your rank as soon as all these computations have been made. This will be done as rapidly as possible.

People who are found to meet the requirements in the announcement are called "eligibles." Their names are put on a list of eligible candidates. An eligible's chances of getting a job depend on how high he stands on this list and how fast agencies are filling jobs from the list.

When a job is to be filled from a list of eligibles, the agency asks for the names of people on the list of eligibles for that job. When the civil service commission receives this request, it sends to the agency the names of the three people highest on this list. Or, if the job to be filled has specialized requirements, the office sends the agency the names of the top three persons who meet these requirements from the general list.

The appointing officer makes a choice from among the three people whose names were sent to him. If the selected person accepts the appointment, the names of the others are put back on the list to be considered for future openings.

That is the rule in hiring from all kinds of eligible lists, whether they are for typist, carpenter, chemist, or something else. For every vacancy, the appointing officer has his choice of any one of the top three eligibles on the list. This explains why the person whose name is on top of the list sometimes does not get an appointment when some of the persons lower on the list do. If the appointing officer chooses the second or third eligible, the No. 1 eligible does not get a job at once, but stays on the list until he is appointed or the list is terminated.

X. HOW TO PASS THE INTERVIEW TEST

The examination for which you applied requires an oral interview test. You have already taken the written test and you are now being called for the interview test – the final part of the formal examination.

You may think that it is not possible to prepare for an interview test and that there are no procedures to follow during an interview. Our purpose is to point out some things you can do in advance that will help you and some good rules to follow and pitfalls to avoid while you are being interviewed.

What is an interview supposed to test?

The written examination is designed to test the technical knowledge and competence of the candidate; the oral is designed to evaluate intangible qualities, not readily measured otherwise, and to establish a list showing the relative fitness of each candidate – as measured against his competitors – for the position sought. Scoring is not on the basis of "right" and "wrong," but on a sliding scale of values ranging from "not passable" to "outstanding." As a matter of fact, it is possible to achieve a relatively low score without a single "incorrect" answer because of evident weakness in the qualities being measured.

Occasionally, an examination may consist entirely of an oral test – either an individual or a group oral. In such cases, information is sought concerning the technical knowledges and abilities of the candidate, since there has been no written examination for this purpose. More commonly, however, an oral test is used to supplement a written examination.

Who conducts interviews?

The composition of oral boards varies among different jurisdictions. In nearly all, a representative of the personnel department serves as chairman. One of the members of the board may be a representative of the department in which the candidate would work. In some cases, "outside experts" are used, and, frequently, a businessman or some other representative of the general public is asked to serve. Labor and management or other special groups may be represented. The aim is to secure the services of experts in the appropriate field.

However the board is composed, it is a good idea (and not at all improper or unethical) to ascertain in advance of the interview who the members are and what groups they represent. When you are introduced to them, you will have some idea of their backgrounds and interests, and at least you will not stutter and stammer over their names.

What should be done before the interview?

While knowledge about the board members is useful and takes some of the surprise element out of the interview, there is other preparation which is more substantive. It *is* possible to prepare for an oral interview – in several ways:

1) Keep a copy of your application and review it carefully before the interview

This may be the only document before the oral board, and the starting point of the interview. Know what education and experience you have listed there, and the sequence and dates of all of it. Sometimes the board will ask you to review the highlights of your experience for them; you should not have to hem and haw doing it.

2) Study the class specification and the examination announcement

Usually, the oral board has one or both of these to guide them. The qualities, characteristics or knowledges required by the position sought are stated in these documents. They offer valuable clues as to the nature of the oral interview. For example, if the job involves supervisory responsibilities, the announcement will usually indicate that knowledge of modern supervisory methods and the qualifications of the candidate as a supervisor will be tested. If so, you can expect such questions, frequently in the form of a hypothetical situation which you are expected to solve. NEVER go into an oral without knowledge of the duties and responsibilities of the job you seek.

3) Think through each qualification required

Try to visualize the kind of questions you would ask if you were a board member. How well could you answer them? Try especially to appraise your own knowledge and background in each area, *measured against the job sought*, and identify any areas in which you are weak. Be critical and realistic – do not flatter yourself.

4) Do some general reading in areas in which you feel you may be weak

For example, if the job involves supervision and your past experience has NOT, some general reading in supervisory methods and practices, particularly in the field of human relations, might be useful. Do NOT study agency procedures or detailed manuals. The oral board will be testing your understanding and capacity, not your memory.

5) Get a good night's sleep and watch your general health and mental attitude

You will want a clear head at the interview. Take care of a cold or any other minor ailment, and of course, no hangovers.

What should be done on the day of the interview?

Now comes the day of the interview itself. Give yourself plenty of time to get there. Plan to arrive somewhat ahead of the scheduled time, particularly if your appointment is in the fore part of the day. If a previous candidate fails to appear, the board might be ready for you a bit early. By early afternoon an oral board is almost invariably behind schedule if there are many candidates, and you may have to wait. Take along a book or magazine to read, or your application to review, but leave any extraneous material in the waiting room when you go in for your interview. In any event, relax and compose yourself.

The matter of dress is important. The board is forming impressions about you – from your experience, your manners, your attitude, and your appearance. Give your personal appearance careful attention. Dress your best, but not your flashiest. Choose conservative, appropriate clothing, and be sure it is immaculate. This is a business interview, and your appearance should indicate that you regard it as such. Besides, being well groomed and properly dressed will help boost your confidence.

Sooner or later, someone will call your name and escort you into the interview room. *This is it.* From here on you are on your own. It is too late for any more preparation. But remember, you asked for this opportunity to prove your fitness, and you are here because your request was granted.

What happens when you go in?

The usual sequence of events will be as follows: The clerk (who is often the board stenographer) will introduce you to the chairman of the oral board, who will introduce you to the other members of the board. Acknowledge the introductions before you sit down. Do not be surprised if you find a microphone facing you or a stenotypist sitting by. Oral interviews are usually recorded in the event of an appeal or other review.

Usually the chairman of the board will open the interview by reviewing the highlights of your education and work experience from your application – primarily for the benefit of the other members of the board, as well as to get the material into the record. Do not interrupt or comment unless there is an error or significant misinterpretation; if that is the case, do not hesitate. But do not quibble about insignificant matters. Also, he will usually ask you some question about your education, experience or your present job – partly to get you to start talking and to establish the interviewing "rapport." He may start the actual questioning, or turn it over to one of the other members. Frequently, each member undertakes the questioning on a particular area, one in which he is perhaps most competent, so you can expect each member to participate in the examination. Because time is limited, you may also expect some rather abrupt switches in the direction the questioning takes, so do not be upset by it. Normally, a board member will not pursue a single line of questioning unless he discovers a particular strength or weakness.

After each member has participated, the chairman will usually ask whether any member has any further questions, then will ask you if you have anything you wish to add. Unless you are expecting this question, it may floor you. Worse, it may start you off on an extended, extemporaneous speech. The board is not usually seeking more information. The question is principally to offer you a last opportunity to present further qualifications or to indicate that you have nothing to add. So, if you feel that a significant qualification or characteristic has been overlooked, it is proper to point it out in a sentence or so. Do not compliment the board on the thoroughness of their examination – they have been sketchy, and you know it. If you wish, merely say, "No thank you, I have nothing further to add." This is a point where you can "talk yourself out" of a good impression or fail to present an important bit of information. Remember, *you close the interview yourself*.

The chairman will then say, "That is all, Mr. _____, thank you." Do not be startled; the interview is over, and quicker than you think. Thank him, gather your belongings and take your leave. Save your sigh of relief for the other side of the door.

How to put your best foot forward

Throughout this entire process, you may feel that the board individually and collectively is trying to pierce your defenses, seek out your hidden weaknesses and embarrass and confuse you. Actually, this is not true. They are obliged to make an appraisal of your qualifications for the job you are seeking, and they want to see you in your best light. Remember, they must interview all candidates and a non-cooperative candidate may become a failure in spite of their best efforts to bring out his qualifications. Here are 15 suggestions that will help you:

1) Be natural – Keep your attitude confident, not cocky

If you are not confident that you can do the job, do not expect the board to be. Do not apologize for your weaknesses, try to bring out your strong points. The board is interested in a positive, not negative, presentation. Cockiness will antagonize any board member and make him wonder if you are covering up a weakness by a false show of strength.

2) Get comfortable, but don't lounge or sprawl

Sit erectly but not stiffly. A careless posture may lead the board to conclude that you are careless in other things, or at least that you are not impressed by the importance of the occasion. Either conclusion is natural, even if incorrect. Do not fuss with your clothing, a pencil or an ashtray. Your hands may occasionally be useful to emphasize a point; do not let them become a point of distraction.

3) Do not wisecrack or make small talk

This is a serious situation, and your attitude should show that you consider it as such. Further, the time of the board is limited – they do not want to waste it, and neither should you.

4) Do not exaggerate your experience or abilities

In the first place, from information in the application or other interviews and sources, the board may know more about you than you think. Secondly, you probably will not get away with it. An experienced board is rather adept at spotting such a situation, so do not take the chance.

5) If you know a board member, do not make a point of it, yet do not hide it

Certainly you are not fooling him, and probably not the other members of the board. Do not try to take advantage of your acquaintanceship – it will probably do you little good.

6) Do not dominate the interview

Let the board do that. They will give you the clues – do not assume that you have to do all the talking. Realize that the board has a number of questions to ask you, and do not try to take up all the interview time by showing off your extensive knowledge of the answer to the first one.

7) Be attentive

You only have 20 minutes or so, and you should keep your attention at its sharpest throughout. When a member is addressing a problem or question to you, give him your undivided attention. Address your reply principally to him, but do not exclude the other board members.

8) Do not interrupt

A board member may be stating a problem for you to analyze. He will ask you a question when the time comes. Let him state the problem, and wait for the question.

9) Make sure you understand the question

Do not try to answer until you are sure what the question is. If it is not clear, restate it in your own words or ask the board member to clarify it for you. However, do not haggle about minor elements.

10) Reply promptly but not hastily

A common entry on oral board rating sheets is "candidate responded readily," or "candidate hesitated in replies." Respond as promptly and quickly as you can, but do not jump to a hasty, ill-considered answer.

11) Do not be peremptory in your answers

A brief answer is proper – but do not fire your answer back. That is a losing game from your point of view. The board member can probably ask questions much faster than you can answer them.

12) Do not try to create the answer you think the board member wants

He is interested in what kind of mind you have and how it works – not in playing games. Furthermore, he can usually spot this practice and will actually grade you down on it.

13) Do not switch sides in your reply merely to agree with a board member

Frequently, a member will take a contrary position merely to draw you out and to see if you are willing and able to defend your point of view. Do not start a debate, yet do not surrender a good position. If a position is worth taking, it is worth defending.

14) Do not be afraid to admit an error in judgment if you are shown to be wrong

The board knows that you are forced to reply without any opportunity for careful consideration. Your answer may be demonstrably wrong. If so, admit it and get on with the interview.

15) Do not dwell at length on your present job

The opening question may relate to your present assignment. Answer the question but do not go into an extended discussion. You are being examined for a *new* job, not your present one. As a matter of fact, try to phrase ALL your answers in terms of the job for which you are being examined.

Basis of Rating

Probably you will forget most of these "do's" and "don'ts" when you walk into the oral interview room. Even remembering them all will not ensure you a passing grade. Perhaps you did not have the qualifications in the first place. But remembering them will help you to put your best foot forward, without treading on the toes of the board members.

Rumor and popular opinion to the contrary notwithstanding, an oral board wants you to make the best appearance possible. They know you are under pressure – but they also want to see how you respond to it as a guide to what your reaction would be under the pressures of the job you seek. They will be influenced by the degree of poise you display, the personal traits you show and the manner in which you respond.

ABOUT THIS BOOK

This book contains tests divided into Examination Sections. Go through each test, answering every question in the margin. We have also attached a sample answer sheet at the back of the book that can be removed and used. At the end of each test look at the answer key and check your answers. On the ones you got wrong, look at the right answer choice and learn. Do not fill in the answers first. Do not memorize the questions and answers, but understand the answer and principles involved. On your test, the questions will likely be different from the samples. Questions are changed and new ones added. If you understand these past questions you should have success with any changes that arise. Tests may consist of several types of questions. We have additional books on each subject should more study be advisable or necessary for you. Finally, the more you study, the better prepared you will be. This book is intended to be the last thing you study before you walk into the examination room. Prior study of relevant texts is also recommended. NLC publishes some of these in our Fundamental Series. Knowledge and good sense are important factors in passing your exam. Good luck also helps. So now study this Passbook, absorb the material contained within and take that knowledge into the examination. Then do your best to pass that exam.

EXAMINATION SECTION

EXAMINATION SECTION
TEST 1

DIRECTIONS: Each question or incomplete statement is followed by several suggested answers or completions. Select the one that BEST answers the question or completes the statement. *PRINT THE LETTER OF THE CORRECT ANSWER IN THE SPACE AT THE RIGHT.*

Questions 1-5.

DIRECTIONS: Questions 1 to 5 refer to the table below.

TABLE 1: NEW HOUSING UNITS STARTED 2000-2005
(Hypothetical)

YEAR	TOTAL IN THOUSANDS	PERCENT CHANGE[1]	PRIVATELY OWNED (in thousands)		PUBLICLY OWNED IN THOUSANDS
			TOTAL	1-UNIT STRUCTURE	
2000	1,398	-20.4	1,250	990	I
2001	II	4.9	1,370	1,120	96
2002	1,524	4.0	III	1,236	104
2003	1,420	-6.8	1,325	1,164	95
2004	1,380	-2.8	1,260	IV	120
2005	1,690	V	1,520	1,415	170

[1]Change from previous year
Minus sign (-) denotes decrease

1. What is the value of I?

    A. 148
    B. 150
    C. 146
    D. 248
    E. None of the above, or cannot be calculated from the data provided

1.____

2. What is the value of II?

    A. 1,216
    B. 2,495
    C. 1,466
    D. 1,464
    E. None of the above, or cannot be calculated from the data provided

2.____

3. What is the value of III?

    A. 288
    B. 1,420
    C. 1,132
    D. 1,430
    E. None of the above, or cannot be calculated from the data provided

3.____

4. What is the value of IV?

   A. 1,140
   B. 1,380
   C. 1,102
   D. 1,094
   E. None of the above, or cannot be calculated from the data provided

5. What is the value of V?

   A. 18.3
   B. 81.7
   C. 21.5
   D. 22.5
   E. None of the above, or cannot be calculated from the data provided

Questions 6-10.

DIRECTIONS: Questions 6 to 10 test the applicant's ability to determine whether or not conclusions are true based on a given set of premises. The examinee should first read the premises that are given; then, look at the conclusion. Assume that the premises are true and decide whether the conclusion is:
   A. Necessarily true
   B. Probably, but not necessarily true
   C. Indeterminable, cannot be determined
   D. Probably, but not necessarily false
   E. Necessarily false

6. *Premises:* If the Commission approves the new proposal, the agency will move to a new location immediately. If the agency moves, five new supervisors will be appointed immediately. The Commission approved the new proposal.

   Conclusion: No new supervisors were appointed.

7. *Premises:* If the director retires, John Jackson, the associate director, will not be transferred to another agency. Jackson will be promoted to director if he is not transferred. The director retired.

   Conclusion: Jackson will be promoted to director.

8. *Premises:* If the maximum allowable income for food stamp recipients is increased, the number of food stamp recipients will increase. If the number of food stamp recipients increases, more funds must be allocated to the food stamp program, which will require a tax increase. Taxes cannot be raised without the approval of Congress. Congress probably will not approve a tax increase.

   Conclusion: The maximum allowable income for food stamp recipients will increase.

9. *Premises:* If prices are raised and sales remain constant, profits will increase. Prices were raised and sales levels will probably be maintained.

   Conclusion: Profits will increase.

   9.____

10. *Premises:* Some employees in the personnel department are technicians. Most of the technicians working in the personnel department are test development specialists. Lisa Jones works in the personnel department.

    Conclusion: Lisa Jones is a technician.

    10.____

Questions 11-15.

DIRECTIONS: Many jobs require skill in analyzing, understanding, and interpreting written material of varying levels of difficulty. These questions are primarily designed to test the applicant's comprehension and interpretation abilities. Therefore, Questions 11 to 15 require examinees to understand a given paragraph and to choose an answer based on their comprehension of the general concept used in the written passage. The right answer is usually a repetition in different terminology of the main concept(s) found in the passage. It may also be a conclusion drawn from the content of the paragraph that is equivalent to a restatement. The applicant should read each passage and select the one of the five statements that is BEST supported by the contents of the passage.

11. *A viable affirmative action program must contain specific procedures designed to achieve equal employment opportunities for specified groups. Appropriate procedures, without necessary determination to carry them out, are useless. Determination, without well-defined procedures, will achieve only partial success.*
    The paragraph BEST supports the statement that:

    11.____

    A. Well-defined procedures will assure the success of an affirmative action program
    B. A high degree of determination is necessary and sufficient for a highly successful affirmative action program
    C. It is impossible for an agency to develop a viable affirmative action program
    D. An agency may guarantee success of its affirmative action program by developing and implementing well-defined procedures
    E. Two important ingredients of a successful affirmative action program are well-defined procedures and a sincere resolve to implement those procedures

12. *Claimants who have become unemployed by voluntarily leaving the job, by refusing to accept suitable work, or due to misconduct should be temporarily disqualified from receiving benefits. However, the disqualification period should never be longer than the average period required for a worker to find employment. Unemployment insurance is designed to alleviate hardship due to unemployment. Benefits should definitely be paid if unemployment continues beyond a certain point and the claimant can show that he has made an honest effort to find employment.*
    The paragraph BEST supports the statement that:

    12.____

    A. If a claimant cannot find work after a certain period of time, he/she should no longer receive benefits
    B. In cases of willful misconduct, disqualification should continue indefinitely
    C. The reasons for unemployment change as the period of unemployment gets longer

D. If a claimant cannot find employment after a certain period of time, he/she should be allowed to receive unemployment insurance benefits
E. If a claimant chooses voluntary unemployment, he/she should receive unemployment insurance benefits immediately

13. *Education in the United States is a state responsibility, a local function, and a federal concern. Unlike other social service programs, this arrangement also places state governments between the federal government and local governing bodies.*
    The paragraph BEST supports the statement that:

    A. Enforcement of federal education policies is left to state discretion
    B. The federal government plays an advisory role only in matters concerning education
    C. Federal educational policies are generally implemented by local governments under the direction of the state
    D. No federal funds are used to support local educational programs
    E. Federal aid is often used to induce local school systems to implement federal policies

13.____

14. *Technological and psychological conditions are changing so rapidly that most agencies and organizations must continually adapt to new situations in order to remain viable.*
    The paragraph BEST supports the statement that:

    A. Changes in general conditions determine the effectiveness of an organization
    B. The effectiveness of an organization depends more on technological advances than on psychological changes
    C. Organizations must be able to adapt to technological and psychological changes in order to maintain effectiveness
    D. The effectiveness of an organization is equally dependent upon technological advances and psychological changes
    E. The effectiveness of an organization is dependent upon its technological and psychological advances

14.____

15. *A disability may be defined as the inability to perform one or more activities essential to normal everyday living. Some examples are basic care of self, earning a living, and social competence. Some basic causes are physical impairment due to illness or injury, mental impairment, and physical or mental deprivation*
    The paragraph BEST supports the statement that a disability is

    A. a term utilized to denote any lessening of an individual's ability to perform normal daily activities
    B. any acute or chronic condition that may be permanent or long-range in nature
    C. any physical or mental impairment which inhibits higher order intellectual pursuits
    D. an acute or chronic condition that can be described by the pathology underlying the condition
    E. defined as the inability to perform any activity essential to normal everyday living

15.____

Questions 16-20.

DIRECTIONS: Many occupations require skill in solving quantitative problems of varying degrees of difficulty. Questions 16 to 20 are designed to test these abilities. Read each statement carefully before attempting to solve the problem.

16. Angela Winston processed 300 applications for food stamps during the month of June. During the month of July, she processed 10% fewer applications. Determine the number she processed in July.   16.____

    A. 220   B. 240   C. 270
    D. 280   E. None of the above

17. A personnel officer drove from Lake Charles to a conference in Baton Rouge. The total distance for the round trip was 240 miles. The time required to travel one way to Baton Rouge was two hours. Due to heavy traffic during the return trip to Lake Charles, an extra hour was required.
    How much *slower* was the personnel officer traveling on the return trip?   17.____

    A. 10 mph   B. 15 mph   C. 20 mph
    D. 25 mph   E. None of the above

18. Ten employment security interviewers interviewed a total of 800 applicants in five days. Sixty percent of those interviewed were placed on jobs.
    If each interviewer worked 8 hours each day, what was the AVERAGE number of applicants placed on jobs each hour by each interviewer?   18.____

    A. 1.2   B. 0.8   C. 0.5
    D. 1.5   E. None of the above

19. A state park *is* budgeted at an amount 9 times the amount budgeted for a nearby city park.
    If the combined yearly budget of both parks is $1,000,000, what is the average monthly budget of the city park?   19.____

    A. $8,111.00   B. $8,222.22   C. $8,333.33
    D. $8,444.44   E.

20. The estimated completion time for a 100-item test is 3 1/3 hours. Ten applicants actually took the test and completed it in 3 hours.
    What is the difference, in seconds, between the actual and estimated rate of completion per item?   20.____

    A. 10   B. 12   C. 14
    D. 16   E. None of the above

KEY (CORRECT ANSWERS)

1.	A	11.	E
2.	C	12.	D
3.	B	13.	C
4.	E	14.	C
5.	D	15.	E
6.	E	16.	C
7.	A	17.	C
8.	D	18.	A
9.	B	19.	C
10.	C	20.	B

SOLUTIONS TO PROBLEMS

1. The answer is 148 or A. The figure represents the number of publicly-owned units which is obtained by subtracting the number of privately-owned units from the total: 1,398 - 1,250 = 148.

2. The answer is 1,466 or C. The figure represents the total number of housing units which is obtained by adding the total number of privately-owned units to the number of publicly-owned units: 1,370 + 96 = 1,466. Alternative A represents the sum of the total number of publicly-owned units and the number of 1-unit, privately-owned structures. Alternatives B and D are irrelevant values.

3. The answer is 1,420 or B. It is obtained by subtracting the number of publicly-owned units from the total number of housing units: 1,524 - 104 = 1,420. Alternative A is obtained by subtracting the number of 1-unit, privately-owned structures from the total number of units. Alternatives C and D are irrelevant values.

4. The answer is E. The number of privately-owned 1-unit structures cannot be calculated since the number of privately-owned multi-unit structures is not given in the table. Alternative A represents the difference between the number of privately-owned units and the number of publicly-owned units. Alternative B represents the sum of publicly-owned units and privately-owned units. Alternatives C and D are irrelevant values.

5. The answer is 22.5 or D. The percent change is calculated by computing the increase or decrease and dividing the result by the number that existed before the change: 1,690 - 1,380 = 310 and 310/1380 = 22.46 or 22.5. Alternative A erroneously divides 310 by 1,690, and Alternative B was found by erroneously dividing 1,380 by 1,690. Alternative C is an irrelevant value.

6. The correct answer is E. The new proposal was approved. According to the premises, approval means that the agency will move, and moving to a new location means that five new supervisors will be appointed.

7. The correct answer is A. According to the premises, the director retired, which means that Jackson will not be transferred and, therefore, will be promoted to director.

8. The correct answer is D (probably, but not necessarily false). Since Congress probably will not approve a tax increase, the maximum allowable income for food stamp recipients probably will not increase.

9. The correct answer is B (probably, but not necessarily true). According to the premises, profits will increase if prices are raised and sales remain constant. It is known that prices were raised. Although sales levels will probably be maintained, this is not certain.

10. The correct answer is C (indeterminable, cannot be determined). The premises give no indication of the proportion of employees who are technicians. Therefore, no conclusion can be drawn with respect to the probability that any one employee is a technician.

11. The correct alternative, E, restates the idea presented in the paragraph. Statements A and B each contain only one of the ingredients. Alternative D overstates the implications of the paragraph.

12. The correct alternative, D, summarizes the meaning of the passage as a whole. Alternative A concerns the length of time the claimant should receive benefits. Alternatives B and E contradict parts of the passage and the idea expressed in Alternative C is not addressed in the paragraph.

13. Correct alternative, C, is supported by the paragraph. The ideas expressed in Alternatives A, B, and D are not addressed in the paragraph. Although Alternative E is probably true, it is not mentioned in the paragraph.

14. Correct alternative, C, effectively restates the essence of the paragraph. In contrast to Alternatives A and B, the paragraph states that organizations must adapt to changes. Alternatives D and E imply that effectiveness of an organization depends on change; however, the paragraph states that effectiveness depends on an organization's ability to adapt to change.

15. Correct alternative E is supported by the first sentence of the paragraph. Alternatives B, C, and D are not supported by the paragraph. Although Alternative A is supported by the paragraph to some extent, its lack of specificity makes it less acceptable than Alternative

16. The answer is C. First, compute 10% of 300: 300 x .10 = 30. Second, subtract the result from 300: 300 - 30 = 270.

17. The answer is C. First, compute the distance one way: 1/2 x 240 = 120 miles. Second, calculate the rate going: 120 miles ÷ 2 hours = 60 mph. Third, calculate the rate returning: 120 miles ÷ 3 hours = 40 mph. Fourth, compute the difference: 60 mph - 40 mph = 20 mph.

18. The answer is A. The total number of applicants placed on jobs equals 60% of 800: .60 x 800 = 480. The total placed per day equals 480 divided by the number of days: 480 ÷ 5 = 96. The total placed per hour equals 96 divided by hours per day: 96 ÷ 8 = 12. The total placed per hour per interviewer equals the total placed per hour divided by the number of interviewers: 12 ÷ 10 = 1.2.

19. The correct answer is C. Let x = the annual city park budget and 9x = the annual state park budget. Therefore, 10x = $1,000,000, and x = $100,000. $100,000 divided by 12 = $8,333.33, the average monthly city park budget.

20. The answer is B. The estimated time per item equals the estimated time divided by the number of items:

$$\frac{3\,1/3 \times 60}{100} = \frac{10/3 \times 60}{100} = \frac{10 \times 20}{100} = \frac{200}{100} = 2 \text{ minutes}$$

The actual time equals 3 hours or 180 minutes. The actual time per item equals 180 minutes divided by the number of items: 180 ÷ 100 = 1.8 minutes. The difference in estimated time and actual time equals 2 minutes minus 1.8 minutes: 2.0 - 1.8 = .2 minutes or .2 x 60 seconds = 12 seconds.

EXAMINATION SECTION
TEST 1

DIRECTIONS: Each question or incomplete statement is followed by several suggested answers or completions. Select the one that BEST answers the question or completes the statement. *PRINT THE LETTER OF THE CORRECT ANSWER IN THE SPACE AT THE RIGHT.*

Questions 1-5.

DIRECTIONS: Each of Questions 1 through 5 consists of a passage which contains one word that is incorrectly used because it is not in keeping with the meaning that the quotation is evidently intended to convey. Determine which word is incorrectly used. Select from the choices lettered A, B, C, and D the word which, when substituted for the incorrectly used word, would BEST to convey the meaning of the quotation.

1. Whatever the method, the necessity to keep up with the dynamics of an organization is the point on which many classification plans go awry. The budgetary approach to "positions," for example, often leads to using for recruitment and pay purposes a position authorized many years earlier for quite a different purpose than currently contemplated—making perhaps the title, the class, and the qualifications required inappropriate to the current need. This happens because executives overlook the stability that takes place in job duties and fail to reread an initial description of the job before saying, as they scan a list of titles, "We should fill this position right away." Once a classification plan is adopted, it is pointless to do anything less than provide for continuous, painstaking maintenance on a current basis, else once different positions that have actually become similar to each other remain in different classes, and some former cognates that have become quite different continue in the same class. Such a program often seems expensive. But to stint too much on this out-of-pocket cost may create still higher hidden costs growing out of lowered morale, poor production, delayed operating programs, excessive pay for simple work, and low pay for responsible work (resulting in poorly qualified executives and professional men)—all normal concomitants of inadequate, hasty, or out-of-date classification. 1.____

   A. evolution   B. personnel   C. disapproved   D. forward

2. At first sight, it may seem that there is little or no difference between the usableness of a manual and the degree of its use. But there is a difference. A manual may have all the qualities which make up the usable manual and still not be used. Take this instance as an example: Suppose you have a satisfactory manual but issue instructions from day to day through the avenue of bulletins, memorandums, and other informational releases. Which will the employee use, the manual or the bulletin which passes over his desk? He will, 2.____

2 (#1)

of course, use the latter, for some obsolete material will not be contained in this manual. Here we have a theoretically usable manual which is unused because of the other avenues by which procedural information may be issued.
    A. countermand   B. discard   C. intentional   D. worthwhile

3. By reconcentrating control over its operations in a central headquarters, a firm is able to extend the influence of automation to many, if not all, of its functions—from inventory and payroll to production, sales, and personnel. In so doing, businesses freeze all the elements of the corporate function in their relationship to one another and to the overall objectives of the firm. From this total systems concept, companies learn that computers can accomplish much more than clerical and accounting jobs. Their capabilities can be tapped to perform the traditional applications (payroll processing, inventory control, accounts payable, and accounts receivable) as well as newer applications such as spotting deviations from planned programs (exception reporting), adjusting planning schedules, forecasting business trends, simulating market conditions, and solving production problems. Since the officer manage is a manager of information and each of these applications revolve around the processing of data, he must take an active role in studying and improving the system under his care.
    A. maintaining   B. inclusion   C. limited   D. visualize

3.____

4. In addition to the formal and acceptance theories of the source of authority, although perhaps more closely related to the latter, is the belief that authority is generated by personal qualifies of technical competence. Under this heading is the individual who has made, in effect, subordinates of others through sheer force of personality, and the engineer or economist who exerts influence by furnishing answers or sound advice. These may have no actual organizational authority, yet their advice may be so eagerly sought and so unerringly followed that it appears to carry the weight of an order. But, above all, one cannot discount the importance of formal authority with its institutional foundations. Buttressed by the qualities of leadership implicit in the acceptance theory, formal authority is basic to the managerial job. Once abrogated, it may be delegated or withheld, used or misused, and be effective in capable hands or be ineffective in inept hands.
    A. selected   B. delegation   C. limited   D. possessed

4.____

5. Since managerial operations in organization, staffing, directing, and controlling are designed to support the accomplishment of enterprise objectives, planning logically precedes the execution of all other managerial functions. Although all the functions intermesh in practice, planning is unique in that it establishes the objectives necessary for all group effort. Besides, plans must be made to accomplish these objectives before the manager knows what kind of organization relationships and personal qualifications are needed, along which course subordinates are to be directed, and what kind of control is to be applied. And, of course, each of the other managerial functions must be planned if they are to be effective.

5.____

Planning and control are inseparable—the Siamese twins of management. Unplanned action cannot be controlled, for control involves keeping activities on course by correcting deviations from plans. Any attempt to control without plans would be meaningless, since there are no way anyone can tell whether he is going where he wants to go—the task of control—unless first he knows where he wants to go—the task of planning. Plans thus preclude the standards of control.

   A. coordinating   B. individual   C. furnish   D. follow

Questions 6-7.

DIRECTIONS: Questions 6 and 7 are to be answered SOLELY on the basis of information given in the following paragraph.

In-basket tests are often used to assess managerial potential. The exercise consists of a set of papers that would be likely to be found in the in-basket of an administrator or manager at any given time, and requires the individuals participating in the examination to indicate how they would dispose of each item found in the in-basket. In order to handle the in-basket effectively, they must successfully manage their time, refer and assign some work to subordinates, juggle potentially conflicting appointments and meetings, and arrange for follow-up of problems generated by the items in the in-basket. In other words, the in-basket test is attempting to evaluate the participants' abilities to organize their work, set priorities, delegate control, and make decisions.

6. According to the above paragraph, to succeed in an in-basket test, an administrator must
   A. be able to read very quickly
   B. have a great deal of technical knowledge
   C. know when to delegate work
   D. arrange a lot of appointments and meetings

6.____

7. According to the above paragraph, all of the following abilities are indications of managerial potential EXCEPT the ability to
   A. organize and control   B. manage time
   C. write effective reports   D. make appropriate decisions

7.____

Questions 8-9.

DIRECTIONS: Questions 8 and 9 are to be answered SOLELY on the basis of information given in the following paragraph.

One of the biggest mistakes of government executives with substantial supervisory responsibility is failing to make careful appraisals of performance during employee probationary periods. Many a later headache could have been avoided by prompt and full appraisal during the early months of an employee's assignment. There is not much more to say about this except to emphasize the common prevalence of this oversight, and to underscore that for its consequences, which are many and sad, the offending managers have no one to blame but themselves.

8. According to the above paragraph, probationary periods are
   A. a mistake, and should not be used by supervisors with large responsibilities
   B. not used properly by government executives
   C. used only for those with supervisory responsibility
   D. the consequences of management mistakes

9. The one of the following conclusions that can MOST appropriately be drawn from the above paragraph is that
   A. management's failure to appraise employees during their probationary period is a common occurrence
   B. there is not much to say about probationary periods, because they are unimportant
   C. managers should blame employees for failing to use their probationary periods properly
   D. probationary periods are a headache to most managers

Questions 10-12.

DIRECTIONS: Questions 11 and 12 are to be answered SOLELY on the basis of the information given in the following paragraph.

The common sense character of the merit system seems so natural to most Americans that many people wonder why it should ever have been inoperative. After all, the American economic system, the most phenomenal the world has ever known, is also founded on a rugged selective process which emphasizes the personal qualities of capacity, industriousness, and productivity. The criteria may not have always been appropriate and competition has not always been fair, but competition there was, and the responsibilities and the rewards—with exceptions, of course—have gone to those who could measure up in terms of intelligence, knowledge, or perseverance. This has been true not only in the economic area, in the money-making process, but also in achievement in the professions and other walks of life.

10. According to the above paragraph, economic awards in the United States have
    A. always been based on appropriate, fair criteria
    B. only recently been based on a competitive system
    C. not gone to people who compete too ruggedly
    D. usually gone to those people with intelligence, knowledge, and perseverance

11. According to the above paragraph, a merit system is
    A. an unfair criterion on which to base rewards
    B. unnatural to anyone who is not American
    C. based only on common sense
    D. based on the same principles as the American economic system

12. According to the above paragraph, it is MOST accurate to say that   12.____
    A. the United States has always had a civil service merit system
    B. civil service employees are very rugged
    C. the American economic system has always been based on a merit objective
    D. competition is unique to the American way of life

Questions 13-15.

DIRECTIONS: The management study of employee absence due to sickness is an effective tool in planning. Questions 13 through 15 are to be answered SOLELY on the data given below.

Number of Days Absent Per Worker (Sickness)	1	2	3	4	5	6	7	8 or Over
Number of Workers	76	23	6	3	1	0	1	0
Total Number of Workers	400							
Period Covered	January 1 – December 31							

13. The total number of man-days lost due to illness was   13.____
    A. 110   B. 137   C. 144   D. 164

14. What percent of the workers had 4 or more days absence due to sickness?   14.____
    A. .25%   B. 2.5%   C. 1.25%   D. 12.5%

15. Of the 400 workers studied, the number who lost no days due to sickness was   15.____
    A. 190   B. 236   C. 290   D. 346

Questions 16-18.

DIRECTIONS: In the graph below, the lines labeled "A" and "B" represent the cumulative progress in the work of two file clerks, each of whom was given 500 consecutively numbered applications to file in the proper cabinets over a five-day work week. Questions 16 through 18 are to be answered SOLELY upon the data provided in the graph.

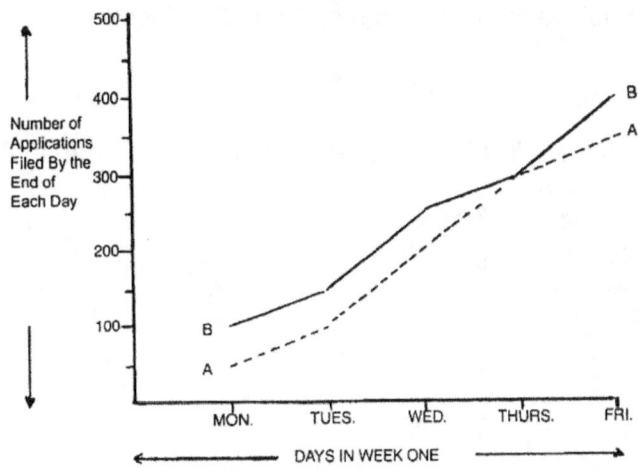

16. The day during which the LARGEST number of applications was filed by both clerks was
    A. Monday   B. Tuesday   C. Wednesday   D. Friday

17. At the end of the second day, the percentage of applications STILL to be filed was
    A. 25%   B. 50%   C. 66%   D. 75%

18. Assuming that the production pattern is the same the following week as the week shown in the chart, the day on which the file clerks will FINISH this assignment will be
    A. Monday   B. Tuesday   C. Wednesday   D. Friday

Questions 19-21.

DIRECTIONS: The following chart shows the differences between the rates of production of employees in Department D in 2009 and 2019. Questions 19 through 21 are to be answered SOLELY on the basis of the information given in the chart.

Number of Employees Producing Work-Units Within Range in 2009	Number of Work-Units Produced	Number of Employees Producing Work-Units Within Range in 2019
7	500 – 1000	4
14	1001 – 1500	11
26	1501 – 2000	28
22	2001 – 2500	36
17	2501 – 3000	39
10	3001 – 3500	23
1	3501 - 4000	9

19. Assuming that within each range of work-units produced the average production was at the mid-point at that range (e.g., category 500 – 1000 = 750), then the AVERAGE number of work-units produced per employee in 2009 fell into the range
    A. 1001 – 1500   B. 1501 – 2000   C. 2001 – 2500   D. 2501 – 3000

20. The ratio of the number of employees producing more than 2000 work-units in 2009 to the number of employees producing more than 2000 work-units in 2019 is MOST NEARLY
    A. 1:2   B. 2:3   C. 3:4   D. 4:5

21. In Department D, which of the following were GREATER in 2019 than in 2009?
    I. Total number of employees
    II. Total number of work-units produced
    III. Number of employees producing 2000 or fewer work-units
    The CORRECT answer is
    A. I, II, III   B. I, II   C. I, III   D. II, III

22. Unit S's production fluctuated substantially from one year to another. In 2018, Unit S's production was 100% greater than in 2017. In 2019, production decreased by 25% from 2018. In 2020, Unit S's production was 10% greater than in 2019.
On the basis of this information, it is CORRECT to conclude that Unit S's production in 2020 exceeded Unit S's production in 2017 by
    A. 65%   B. 85%   C. 95%   D. 135%

22.____

23. Agency "X" is moving into a new building. It has 1500 employees presently on its staff and does not contemplate much variance from this level. The new building contains 100 available offices, each with a maximum capacity of 30 employees. It has been decided that only 2/3 of the maximum capacity of each office will be utilized.
The TOTAL number of offices that will be occupied by Agency "X" is
    A. 30   B. 66   C. 75   D. 90

23.____

24. One typist completes a form letter every 5 minutes and another typist completes one every 6 minutes.
If the two typists start together, they will again start typing new letters simultaneously _____ minutes later and will have completed _____ letters by that time.
    A. 11; 30   B. 12; 24   C. 24; 12   D. 30; 11

24.____

25. During one week, a machine operator produces 10 fewer pages per hour of work than he usually does.
If it ordinarily takes him six hours to produce a 300-page report, it will take him _____ hours longer to produce that same 300-page report during the week when he produces more slowly.
    A. 1½   B. 1²/₃   C. 2   D. 2¾

25.____

KEY (CORRECT ANSWERS)

		Incorrect Words
1.	A	stability
2.	D	obsolete
3.	D	freeze
4.	D	abrogated
5.	C	preclude

6.	C	16.	C
7.	C	17.	D
8.	B	18.	B
9.	A	19.	C
10.	D	20.	A
11.	D	21.	B
12.	C	22.	A
13.	D	23.	C
14.	C	24.	D
15.	C	25.	A

EXAMINATION SECTION
TEST 1

DIRECTIONS: Each question or incomplete statement is followed by several suggested answers or completions. Select the one that BEST answers the question or completes the statement. *PRINT THE LETTER OF THE CORRECT ANSWER IN THE SPACE AT THE RIGHT.*

Questions 1-5.

DIRECTIONS: Questions 1 through 5 consist of sentences, each of which contains one underlined word whose meaning you are to identify by marking your answer either A, B, C, or D.
EXAMPLE

Public employees should avoid <u>unethical</u> conduct.
The word unethical, as used in the sentence, means MOST NEARLY
   A. fine   B. dishonest   C. polite   D. sleepy
The correct answer is *dishonest* (B). Therefore, you should mark your answer B.

1. Employees who can produce a <u>considerable</u> amount of good work are very valuable.   1.____
   The word *considerable*, as used in the sentence, means MOST NEARLY
      A. large   B. potential   C. necessary   D. frequent

2. No person should <u>assume</u> that he knows more than anyone else.   2.____
   The word *assume*, as used in the sentence, means MOST NEARLY
      A. verify   B. hope   C. suppose   D. argue

3. The parties decided to <u>negotiate</u> through the night.   3.____
   The word *negotiate*, as used in the sentence, means MOST NEARLY
      A. suffer   B. play   C. think   D. bargain

4. Employees who have <u>severe</u> emotional problems may create problems at work.   4.____
   The word *severe*, as used in the sentence, means MOST NEARLY
      A. serious   B. surprising   C. several   D. common

5. Supervisors should try to be as <u>objective</u> as possible when dealing with subordinates.   5.____
   The word *objective*, as used in the sentence, means MOST NEARLY
      A. pleasant   B. courteous   C. fair   D. strict

Questions 6-10.

DIRECTIONS: In each of Questions 6 through 10, one word is wrong because it is NOT in keeping with the intended meaning of the statement. First, decide which word is wrongly used; then select as your answer the right word which really belongs in its place.

EXAMPLE

The employee told ill and requested permission to leave early.
  A. felt   B. considered   C. cried   D. spoke

The word "*told*" is clearly wrong and not in keeping with the intended meaning of the quotation.
The word "*felt*" (A), however, would clearly convey the intended meaning of the sentence. Option A is correct. Your answer space, therefore, should be marked A.

6. Only unwise supervisors would deliberately overload their subordinates in order to create themselves look good.
  A. delegate   B. make   C. reduce   D. produce

7. In a democratic organization each employee is seen as a special individual kind of fair treatment.
  A. granted   B. denial   C. perhaps   D. deserving

8. In order to function the work flow in an office you should begin by identifying each important procedure being performed in that office.
  A. uniformity   B. study   C. standards   D. reward

9. A wise supervisor tries to save employees' time by simplifying forms or adding forms where possible.
  A. taxing   B. supervising   C. eliminating   D. protecting

10. A public agency, whenever it changes its program, should give requirements to the need for retraining its employees.
  A. legislation   B. consideration
  C. permission   D. advice

Questions 11-15.

DIRECTIONS: Questions 11 through 15 are to be answered ONLY on the basis of the reading passage preceding each question.

11. Things may not always be what they seem to be. Thus, the wise supervisor should analyze his problems and determine whether there is something there that does not meet the eye. For example, what may seem on the surface to be a personality clash between two subordinates may really be a problem of faulty organization, bad communication, or bad scheduling.

3 (#1)

Which one of the following statements BEST supports this passage?
A. The wise supervisor should avoid personality clashes.
B. The smart supervisor should figure out what really is going on.
C. Bad scheduling is the result of faulty organization.
D. The best supervisor is the one who communicates effectively.

12. Some supervisors, under the pressure of meeting deadlines, become harsh and dictatorial to their subordinates. However, the supervisor most likely to be effective in meeting deadlines is one who absorbs or cushions pressures from above.
According to the passage, if a supervisor wishes to meet deadlines, it is MOST important that he
A. be informative to his superiors
B. encourage personal initiative among his subordinates
C. become harsh and dictatorial to his subordinates
D. protects his subordinates from pressures from above

12.____

13. When giving instructions, a supervisor must always make clear his meaning, leaving no room for misunderstanding. For example, a supervisor who tells a subordinate to do a task "as soon as possible" might legitimately be understood to mean either "it's top priority" or "do it when you can."
Which of the following statements is BEST supported by the passage?
A. Subordinates will attempt to avoid work by deliberately distorting instructions.
B. Instructions should be short, since brief instructions are the clearest.
C. Less educated subordinates are more likely to honestly misunderstand instructions.
D. A supervisor should give precise instructions that cannot be misinterpreted.

13.____

14. Practical formulas are often suggested to simplify what a supervisor should know and how he should behave, such as the four F's (be firm, fair, friendly, and factual). But such simple formulas are really broad principles, not necessarily specific guides in a real situation.
According to the passage, simple formulas for supervisory behavior
A. are superior to complicated theories and principles
B. not always of practical use in actual situations
C. useful only if they are fair and factual
D. would be better understood if written in clear language

14.____

15. Many management decisions are made far removed from the actual place of operations. Therefore, there is a great need for reliable reports and records and, the larger the organization, the greater is the need for such reports and records.
According to the passage, management decisions made far from the place of operations are
A. dependent to a great extent on reliable reports and records
B. sometimes in error because of the great distances involved

15.____

19

C. generally unreliable because of poor communications
D. generally more accurate than on-the-scene decisions

16. Assume that you have just been advanced to a supervisory administrative position and have been assigned as supervisor to a new office with subordinates you do not know.
The BEST way for you to establish good relations with these new subordinates would be to
    A. announce that all actions of the previous supervisor are now cancelled
    B. hold a meeting and warn them that you will not tolerate loafing on the job
    C. reassign all your subordinates to new tasks on the theory that a thorough shake-up is good for morale
    D. act fairly and show helpful interest in their work

16.____

17. One of your subordinates asks you to let her arrive at work 15 minutes later than usual but leave for the day 15 minutes later than she usually does. This is temporarily necessary, your subordinate states, because of early morning medication she must give her sick child.
Which of the following would be the MOST appropriate action for you to take?
    A. Suggest to your subordinate that she choose another family doctor
    B. Warn your subordinate that untruthful excuses are not acceptable
    C. Tell your subordinate that you will consider the request and let her know very shortly
    D. Deny the request since late arrival at work interferes with work performance

17.____

18. A young newly-hired employee asked his supervisor several times for advice on private financial matters. The supervisor commented, in a friendly manner, that he considered it undesirable to give such advice
The supervisor's response was
    A. *unwise*; the supervisor missed an opportunity to advise the employee on an important matter
    B. *wise*; if the financial advice was wrong, it could damage the supervisor's relationship with the subordinate
    C. *unwise*; the subordinate will take up the matter with his fellow workers and probably get poor advice
    D. *wise*; the supervisor should never advise subordinates on any matter

18.____

19. Which of the following is the MOST justified reason for a supervisor to pay any serious attention to a subordinate's off-the-job behavior? The
    A. subordinate's lifestyle is different from the supervisor's way of life
    B. subordinate has become well-known as a serious painter of fine art
    C. subordinate's work has become very poor as a result of his or her personal problems
    D. subordinate is a reserved person who, at work, seldom speaks of personal matters

19.____

20. One of your subordinates complains to you that you assign him to the least pleasant jobs more often than anyone else. You are disturbed by this complaint since you believe you have always rotated such assignments on a fair basis.
Of the following, it would be BEST for you to tell the complaining subordinate that
   A. you will review your past assignment records and discuss the matter with him further
   B. complaints to supervisors are not the wise way to get ahead on the job
   C. disciplinary action will follow if the complaint is not justified
   D. he may be correct, but you do not have sufficient time to verify the complaint

21. Assume that you have called one of your subordinates into your office to talk about the increasing number of careless errors in her work. Until recently, this subordinate had been doing good work, but this is no longer so. Your subordinate does not seem to respond to your questions about the reason for her poor work.
In these circumstances, your NEXT step should be to tell her
   A. that her continued silence will result in severe disciplinary action
   B. to request an immediate transfer from your unit
   C. to return when she is ready to respond
   D. to be more open with you so that her work problem can be identified

22. Assume that you are given a complicated assignment with a tight deadline set by your superior. Shortly after you begin work you realize that, if you are to do a top quality job, you cannot possibly meet the deadline.
In these circumstances, what should be your FIRST course of action?
   A. Continue working as rapidly as possible, hoping that you will meet the deadline after all
   B. Request the assignment be given to an employee whom you believe works faster
   C. Advise your superior of the problem and see whether the deadline can be extended
   D. Advise your superior that the deadline cannot be met and, therefore, you will not start the job

23. Assume that a member of the public comes to you to complain about a long-standing practice of your agency. The complaint seems to be justified.
Which one of the following is the BEST way for you to handle this situation?
   A. Inform the complainant that you will have the agency practice looked into and that he will be advised of any action taken
   B. Listen politely, express sympathy, and state that you see no fault in the practice
   C. Express agreement with the practice on the ground that it has been in effect for many years
   D. Advise the complainant that things will work out well in good time

24. One of your subordinates tells you that he sees no reason for having departmental safety rules.
    Which one of the following replies would be BEST for you to make?
    A. Rules are meant to be obeyed without question
    B. All types of rules are equally important
    C. Safety rules are meant to protect people from injury
    D. If a person is careful enough, he doesn't have to observe safety rules

25. Assume that a supervisor, when he issues instructions to his subordinates, usually names his superior as the source of these instructions.
    This practice is GENERALLY
    A. *wise*, since if things go wrong, the subordinates will know whom to blame
    B. *unwise*, since it may give the subordinates the impression that the supervisor doesn't really support the instructions
    C. *wise*, since it clearly invites the subordinates to go to higher authority if they don't like the instructions

KEY (CORRECT ANSWERS)

1.	A		11.	B
2.	C		12.	D
3.	D		13.	D
4.	A		14.	B
5.	C		15.	A
6.	B		16.	D
7.	D		17.	C
8.	B		18.	B
9.	C		19.	C
10.	B		20.	A

21. D
22. C
23. A
24. C
25. B

TEST 2

DIRECTIONS: Each question or incomplete statement is followed by several suggested answers or completions. Select the one that BEST answers the question or completes the statement. *PRINT THE LETTER OF THE CORRECT ANSWER IN THE SPACE AT THE RIGHT.*

1. An office aide is assigned as a receptionist in a busy office. The office aide often has stretches of idle time between visitors.
   In this situation, the supervisor should
   A. give the receptionist non-urgent clerical jobs which can quickly be done at the reception desk
   B. offer all office aides an opportunity to volunteer for this assignment
   C. eliminate the receptionist assignment
   D. continue the arrangement unchanged, because receptionist duties are so important nothing should interfere with them

   1.____

2. A supervisor can MOST correctly assume that an employee is not performing up to his usual standard when the employee does not handle a task as skillfully as
   A. do other employees who have received less training
   B. do similar employees having comparable work experience
   C. he has handled it in several recent instances
   D. the supervisor himself could handle it

   2.____

3. Assume that you receive a suggestion that you direct all the typists in a typing pool to complete the identical quantity of work each day.
   For you to adopt this suggestion would be
   A. *advisable*; it will demonstrate the absence of supervisory favoritism
   B. *advisable*; all employees in a given title should be treated identically
   C. *inadvisable*; a supervisor should decide on work standards without interference from others
   D. *inadvisable*; it ignores variations in specific assignments and individual skills

   3.____

4. A certain supervisor encouraged her subordinates to tell her if they become aware of possible job problems.
   This practice is good MAINLY because
   A. early awareness of job problems allows more time for seeking solutions
   B. such expected job problems may not develop
   C. the supervisor will be able to solve the job problem without consulting other people
   D. the supervisor will be able to place responsibility for poor work

   4.____

5. Some supervisors will discuss with a subordinate how he is doing on the job only when indicating his mistakes or faults.
   Which of the following is the MOST likely result of such a practice?
   A. The subordinate will become discouraged and frustrated.
   B. Management will set work standards too low.

   5.____

23

C. The subordinate will be favorably impressed by the supervisor's frankness.
D. Supervisors will avoid creating any impression of favoritism.

6. A supervisor calls in a subordinate he supervises to discuss the subordinate's annual work performance, indicating his work deficiencies and also praising his job strengths. The subordinate nods his head as if in agreement with his supervisor's comments on both his strengths and weaknesses, but actually says nothing, even after the supervisor has completed his comments.
At this point, the supervisor should
   A. end the session and assume that the subordinate agrees completely with the evaluation
   B. end the session, since all the subordinate's good and bad points have been identified
   C. ask the supervisor whether the criticism is justified, and, if so, what he, the supervisor, can do to help
   D. thank the subordinate for being so fair-minded in accepting the criticism in a positive manner

7. The successful supervisor is often one who gives serious attention to his subordinates' needs for job satisfaction.
A supervisor who believes this statement is MOST likely to
   A. treat all subordinates in an identical manner, irrespective of individual differences
   B. permit each subordinate to perform his work as he wishes, within reasonable limits
   C. give all subordinates both criticism and praise in equal measure
   D. provide each subordinate with as much direct supervision as possible

8. Assume that you are supervising seven subordinates and have been asked by your superior to prepare an especially complex report due today. Its completion will take the rest of the day. You break down the assignment into simple parts and give a different part to each subordinate.
If you were to explain the work of each subordinate to more than one subordinate, your decision would be
   A. *wise*; this would prevent boredom
   B. *unwise*; valuable time would be lost
   C. *wise*; your subordinates would become well-rounded
   D. *unwise*; your subordinates would lose their competitive spirit

9. Suppose that an office associate whom you supervise has given you a well-researched report on a problem in an area in which he is expert. However, the report lacks solutions or recommendations. You know this office associate to be fearful of stating his opinions.
In these circumstances, you should tell him that
   A. you will seek recommendations on the problem from other, even if less expert, office associates
   B. his work is satisfactory, in hope of arousing him to greater assertiveness

3 (#2)

    C. you need his advice and expertise, to help you reach a decision on the problem
    D. his uncooperative behavior leaves you no choice but to speak to your superior

10. If a supervisor wishes to have the work of his unit completed on schedule, it is usually MOST important to
    A. avoid listening to employees' complaints, thereby discouraging dissatisfaction
    B. perform much of the work himself, since he is generally more capable
    C. observe employees continuously, so they do not slacken their efforts
    D. set up the work carefully, then stay informed as to how it is moving

11. Of the following agencies, the one MOST likely to work out a proposed budget close to its real needs is
    A. a newly-created agency staffed by inexperienced administrators
    B. funded with a considerable amount of money
    C. an existing agency which intends to install new, experimental systems for doing its work
    D. an existing agency which can base its estimate on its experience during the past few years

12. Assume that you are asked to prepare a report on the expected costs and benefits of a proposed new program to be installed in your office. However, you are aware that certain factors are not really measurable in dollars and cents.
As a result, you should
    A. identify the non-measurable factors and state why they are important
    B. assign a fixed money value to all factors that are not really measurable
    C. recommend that programs containing non-measurable factors should be dropped
    D. assume that the non-measurable factors are really unimportant

13. Assume that you are asked for your opinion as to the necessity for hiring more employees to perform certain revenue-producing work in your office.
The information that you will MOST likely need in giving an informed opinion is
    A. whether public opinion would favor hiring additional employees
    B. an estimate of the probable additional revenue compared with the additional personnel costs
    C. the total cost of all city operations in contrast to all city revenues
    D. the method by which present employees would be selected for promotion in an expanded operation

14. The MOST reasonable number of subordinate for a supervisor to have is BEST determined by the
    A. average number of subordinates other supervisors have
    B. particular responsibilities given to the supervisor
    C. supervisor's educational background
    D. personalities of the subordinates assigned to the supervisor

15. Most subordinates would need less supervision if they knew what they were supposed to do.
An ESSENTIAL first step in fixing in subordinates' minds exactly what is required of them is to
    A. require that supervisors be firm in their supervision of subordinates
    B. encourage subordinates to determine their own work standards
    C. encourage subordinates to submit suggestions to improve procedures
    D. standardize and simplify procedures and logically schedule activities

16. Assume that you have been asked to recommend an appropriate office layout to correspond with a just completed office reorganization.
Which of the following is it MOST advisable to recommend?
    A. Allocate most of the space for traffic flow
    B. Use the center area only for traffic flow
    C. Situate close to each other those units whose work is closely related
    D. Group in an out-of-the-way corner the supply and file cabinets

17. Although an organization chart will illustrate the formal structure of an agency, it will seldom show a true picture of its actual workings.
Which of the following BEST explains this statement?
Organization charts
    A. are often prepared by employees who may exaggerate their own importance
    B. usually show titles and sometimes names rather than the actual contacts and movements between employees
    C. are likely to discourage the use of official titles, and in so doing promote greater freedom in human relations
    D. usually show the informal arrangements and dealings between employees

18. Assume that a supervisor of a large unit has a variety of tasks to perform, and that he gives each of his subordinates just one set of tasks to do. He never rotates subordinates from one set of tasks to another.
Which one of the following is the MOST likely advantage to be gained by this practice?
    A. Each subordinate will get to know all the tasks of the unit.
    B. The subordinate will be encouraged to learn all they can about all the unit's tasks.
    C. Each subordinate will become an expert in his particular set of tasks.
    D. The subordinates will improve their opportunities for promotion.

19. Listed below are four steps commonly used in trying to solve administrative problems. These four steps are not listed in the order in which they normally would be taken. If they were listed in the proper order, which step should be taken FIRST?
    I. Choosing the most practical solution to the problem
    II. Analyzing the essential facts about the problem
    III. Correctly identifying the problem
    IV. Following up to see if the solution chosen really works

5 (#2)

The CORRECT answer is:
A. III B. I C. II D. IV

20. Assume that another agency informally tells you that most of your agency's reports are coming to them with careless errors made by many of your office aides.
Which one of the following is MOST likely to solve this problem?
    A. Require careful review of all outgoing reports by the supervisors of the office aides
    B. Request the other agency to make necessary corrections whenever such errors come to their attention
    C. Ask the other agency to submit a written report on this situation
    D. Establish a small unit to review all reports received from other agencies

20.____

21. Assume that you supervise an office which gets two kinds of work. One kind is high-priority and must be done within two days. The other kind of work must be done within two weeks.
Which one of the following instructions would be MOST reasonable for you to give to your subordinates in this office?
    A. If a backlog builds up during the day, clean the backlog up first, regardless of priority
    B. Spend half the day doing priority work and the other half doing non-priority work
    C. Generally do the priority work first as soon as it is received
    D. Usually do the work in the order in which it comes in, priority or non-priority

21.____

22. An experienced supervisor should do advance planning of his subordinates' work assignments and schedules.
Which one of the following is the BEST reason for such advance planning?
It
    A. enables the supervisor to do less supervision
    B. will assure the assignment of varied duties
    C. will make certain a high degree of discipline among subordinates
    D. helps make certain that essential operations are adequately covered

22.____

23. Agencies are required to evaluate the performance of their employees.
Which one of the following would generally be POOR evaluation practice by an agency rater?
The rater
    A. regularly observes the performance of the employee being rated
    B. in evaluating the employee, acquaints himself with the employee's job
    C. uses objective standards in evaluating the employee being rated
    D. uses different standards in evaluating men and women

23.____

24. A good supervisor should have a clear idea of the quantity and quality of his subordinates' work.
Which one of the following sources would normally provide a supervisor with the LEAST reliable information about a subordinate's work performance?
   A. Discussion with a friend of the subordinate
   B. Comments by other supervisors who have worked recently with the subordinate
   C. Opinions of fellow workers who work closely with the subordinate on a daily basis
   D. Comparison with work records of others doing similar work during the same period of time

25. In order to handle the ordinary work of an office, a supervisor sets up standard work procedures.
The MOST likely benefit of this is to reduce the need to
   A. motivate employees to do superior work
   B. rethink what has to be done every time a routine matter comes up
   C. keep record and write reports
   D. change work procedures as new situations come up

KEY (CORRECT ANSWERS)

1.	A		11.	D
2.	C		12.	A
3.	D		13.	B
4.	A		14.	B
5.	A		15.	D
6.	C		16.	C
7.	B		17.	B
8.	B		18.	C
9.	C		19.	A
10.	D		20.	A

21. C
22. D
23. D
24. A
25. B

EXAMINATION SECTION
TEST 1

DIRECTIONS: Each question or incomplete statement is followed by several suggested answers or completions. Select the one that BEST answers the question or completes the statement. *PRINT THE LETTER OF THE CORRECT ANSWER IN THE SPACE AT THE RIGHT.*

1. In almost every organization there is a nucleus of highly important functions commonly designated as *management*.
   Which of the following statements BEST characterizes *management*?
   A. Getting things done through others
   B. The highest level of intelligence in any organization
   C. The process whereby democratic and participative activities are maximized
   D. The *first among equals*

2. Strategies in problem-solving are important to anyone aspiring to advancement in the field of administration.
   Which of the following is BEST classified as the first step in the process of problem-solving?
   A. Collection and organization of data
   B. The formulation of a plan
   C. The definition of the problem
   D. The development of a method and methodology

3. One of the objectives of preparing a budget is to
   A. create optimistic goals which each department can attempt to meet
   B. create an overall company goals by combining the budgets of the various departments
   C. be able to compare planned expenditures against actual expenditures
   D. be able to identify accounting errors

4. The rise in demand for *systems* personnel in industrial and governmental organizations over the past five years has been extraordinary.
   In which of the following areas would a *systems* specialist assigned to an agency be LEAST likely to be of assistance?
   A. Developing, recommending, and establishing an effective cost and inventory system
   B. Development and maintenance of training manuals
   C. Reviewing existing work procedures and recommending improvements
   D. Development of aptitude tests for new employees

5. Management experts have come to the conclusion that the traditional forms of motivation used in industry and government, which emphasize authority over and economic rewards for the employee, are no longer appropriate.

To which of the following factors do such experts attribute the GREATEST importance in producing this change?
   A. The desire of employees to satisfy material needs has become greater and more complex.
   B. The desire for social satisfaction has become the most important aspect of the job for the average worker.
   C. With greater standardization of work processes, there has been an increase in the willingness of workers to accept discipline.
   D. In general, employee organizations have made it more difficult for management to fire an employee.

6. In preparing a budget, it is usually considered advisable to start the initial phases of preparation at the operational level of management.
Of the following, the justification that management experts usually advance as MOST reasonable for this practice is that operating managers, as a consequence of their involvement, will
   A. develop a background in finance or accounting
   B. have an understanding of the organizational structure
   C. tend to feel responsible for carrying out budget activities
   D. have the ability to see the overall financial picture

7. An administrative officer has been asked by his superior to write a concise, factual report with objective conclusions and recommendations based on facts assembled by other researchers.
Of the following factors, the administrative officer should give LEAST consideration to
   A. the educational level of the person or persons for whom the report is being prepared
   B. the use to be made of the report
   C. the complexity of the problem
   D. his own feelings about the importance of the problem

8. In an agency, upon which of the following is a supervisor's effectiveness MOST likely to depend?
The
   A. degree to which a supervisor allows subordinates to participate in the decision-making process and the setting of objectives
   B. degree to which a supervisor's style meets management's objectives and subordinates' needs
   C. strength and forcefulness of the supervisor in pursuing his objectives
   D. expertise and knowledge of the supervisor has about the specific work to be done

9. For authority to be effective, which of the following is the MOST basic requirement?
Authority must be
   A. absolute   B. formalized   C. accepted   D. delegated

10. Management no longer abhors the idea of employees taking daily work breaks, but prefers to schedule such breaks rather than to allot to each employee a standard amount of free time to be taken off during the day as he wishes. Which of the following BEST expresses the reason management theorists give for the practice of scheduling such breaks?
    A. Many jobs fall into natural work units which are scheduled, and the natural time to take a break is at the end of the unit
    B. Taking a scheduled break permits socialization and a feeling of accomplishment
    C. Managers have concluded that scheduling rest periods seems to reduce the incidence of unscheduled ones
    D. Many office workers who really need such breaks are hesitant about taking them unless they are scheduled

11. The computer represents one of the major developments of modern technology. It is widely used in both scientific and managerial activities because of its many advantages.
    Which of the following is NOT an advantage gained by management in the use of the computer?
    A computer
    A. provides the manager with a greatly enlarged memory so that he can easily be provided with data for decision making
    B. relieves the manager of basic decision-making responsibility, thereby giving him more time for directing and controlling
    C. performs routine, repetitive calculations with greater precision and reliability than employees
    D. provides a capacity for rapid simulations of alternative solutions to problem solving

12. A supervisor of a unit in a division is usually responsible for all of the following EXCEPT
    A. the conduct of subordinates in the achievement of division objectives
    B. maintaining quality standards in the unit
    C. the protection and care of materials and equipment in the unit
    D. performing the most detailed tasks in the unit himself

13. You have been assigned to teach a new employee the functions and procedures of your office.
    In your introductory talk, which of the following approaches is PREFERABLE?
    A. Advise the new employee of the employee benefits and services available to him, over and above his salary
    B. Discuss honestly the negative aspects of departmental procedures and indicate methods available to overcome them
    C. Give the new employee an understanding of the general purpose of office procedures and functions and of their relevance to departmental objectives
    D. Give a basic and detailed explanation of the operations of your office, covering all functions and procedures

14. It is your responsibility to assign work to several clerks under your supervision. One of the clerks indignantly refuses to accept an assignment and asks to be given something else. He has not yet indicated why he does not want the assignment, but is sitting there glaring at you, awaiting your reaction.
Of the following, which is the FIRST action you should take?
    A. Ask the employee into your office in order to reprimand him and tell him emphatically that he must accept the assignment
    B. Talk to the employee privately in an effort to find the reason for his indignation and refusal, and then base your action upon your findings
    C. Let the matter drop for a day or two to allow the employee to cool off before you insist that he accept the assignment
    D. Inform the employee quietly and calmly that as his supervisor you have selected him for this assignment and that you fully expect him to accept it

15. Administrative officers are expected to be able to handle duties delegated to them by their supervisors and to be able, as they advance in status, to delegate tasks to assistants.
When considering whether to delegate tasks to a subordinate, which of the following questions should be LEAST important to an administrative officer?
In the delegated tasks,
    A. how significant are the decisions to be made, and how much consultation will be involved?
    B. to what extent is uniformity and close coordination of activity required?
    C. to what extent must speedy-on-the-spot decisions be made?
    D. to what extent will delegation relieve the administrative officer of his burden of responsibility?

16. A functional forms file is a collection of forms which are grouped by
    A. purpose   B. department   C. title   D. subject

17. All of the following are reasons to consult a records retention schedule except one.
Which one is that?
To determine
    A. whether something should be filed
    B. how long something should stay in file
    C. who should be assigned to filing
    D. when something on file should be destroyed

18. Listed below are four of the steps in the process of preparing correspondence for filing.
If they were to be put in logical sequence, the SECOND step would be
    A. preparing cross-reference sheets or cards
    B. coding the correspondence using a classification system
    C. sorting the correspondence in the order to be filed
    D. checking for follow-up action required and preparing a follow-up slip

19. New material added to a file folder should USUALLY be inserted
    A. in the order of importance (the most important in front)
    B. in the order of importance (the most important in back)
    C. chronologically (most recent in front)
    D. chronologically (most recent in back)

20. An individual is looking for a name in the white pages of a telephone directory. Which of the following BEST describes the system of filing found there?
    A(n) _____ file
    A. alphabetic   B. sequential   C. locator   D. index

21. The MAIN purpose of a tickler file is to
    A. help prevent overlooking matters that require future attention
    B. check on adequacy of past performance
    C. pinpoint responsibility for recurring daily tasks
    D. reduce the volume of material kept in general files

22. Which of the following BEST describes the process of reconciling a bank statement?
    A. Analyzing the nature of the expenditures made by the office during the preceding month
    B. Comparing the statement of the bank with the banking records maintained in the office
    C. Determining the liquidity position by reading the bank statement carefully
    D. Checking the service charges noted on the bank statement

23. From the viewpoint of preserving agency or institutional funds, which of the following is the LEAST acceptable method for making a payment?
    A check made out to
    A. cash   B. a company
    C. an individual   D. a partnership

24. In general, the CHIEF economy of using multicopy forms is in
    A. the paper on which the form is printed
    B. printing the form
    C. employee time
    D. carbon paper

25. Suppose your supervisor has asked you to develop a form to record certain information needed.
    The FIRST thing you should do is to
    A. determine the type of data that will be recorded repeatedly so that it can be preprinted
    B. study the relationship of the form to the job to be accomplished so that the form can be planned
    C. determine the information that will be recorded in the same place on each copy of the form so that it can be used as a check
    D. find out who will be responsible for supplying the information so that space can be provided for their signatures

26. An administrative officer in charge of a small fund for buying office supplies has just written a check to Charles Laird, a supplier, and has sent the check by messenger to him. A half-hour later, the messenger telephones the administrative officer. He has lost the check.
Which of the following is the MOST important action for the administrative officer to take under these circumstances?
    A. Ask the messenger to return and write a report describing the loss of the check
    B. Make a note on the performance record of the messenger who lost the check
    C. Take the necessary steps to have payment stopped on the check
    D. Refrain from doing anything since the check may be found shortly

27. A petty cash fund is set up PRIMARILY to
    A. take care of small investments that must be made from time to time
    B. take care of small expenses that arise from time to time
    C. provide a fund to be used as the office wants to use it with little need to maintain records
    D. take care of expenses that develop during emergencies, such as machine breakdowns and fires

28. Of the following, which is usually the MOST important guideline in writing business letters?
A letter should be
    A. neat
    B. written in a formalized style
    C. written in clear language intelligible to the reader
    D. written in the past tense

29. Suppose you are asked to edit a policy statement. You note that personal pronouns like *you*, *we*, and *I* are used freely.
Which of the following statements BEST applies to this use of personal pronouns?
It
    A. is proper usage because written business language should not be different from carefully spoken business language
    B. requires correction because is it ungrammatical
    C. is proper because it is clearer and has a warmer tone
    D. requires correction because policies should be expressed in an impersonal manner

30. Good business letters are coherent.
To be coherent means to
    A. keep only one unifying idea in the message
    B. present the total message
    C. use simple, direct words for the message
    D. tie together the various ideas in the message

31. Proper division of a letter into paragraphs requires that the writer of business letters should, as much as possible, be sure that
    A. each paragraph is short
    B. each paragraph develops discussion of just one topic
    C. each paragraph repeats the theme of the total message
    D. there are at least two paragraphs for every message

31.____

32. An editor is given a letter with this initial paragraph:
    We have received your letter, which we read with interest, and we are happy to respond to your question. In fact, we talked with several people in our office to get ideas to send to you.
    Which of the following is MOST reasonable for the editor to conclude?
    The paragraph is
    A. concise
    B. communicating something of value
    C. unnecessary
    D. coherent

32.____

33. As soon as you pick up the phone, a very angry caller begins immediately to complain about city agencies and *red tape*. He says that he has been shifted to two or three different offices. It turns out that he is seeking information which is not immediately available to you. You believe you know, however, where it can be found.
    Which of the following actions is the BEST one for you to take?
    A. To eliminate all confusion, suggest that the caller write the mayor stating explicitly what he wants
    B. Apologize by telling the caller how busy city agencies now are, but also tell him directly that you do not have the information he needs
    C. Ask for the caller's telephone number and assure him you will call back after you have checked further
    D. Give the caller the name and telephone number of the person who might be able to help, but explain that you are not positive he will get results

33.____

34. Suppose that one of your duties is to dictate responses to routine requests from the public for information. A letter writer asks for information which, as expressed in a one-sentence, explicit agency rule, cannot be given out to the public.
    Of the following ways of answering the letter, which is the MOST efficient?
    A. Quote verbatim that section of the agency rules which prohibit giving this information to the public
    B. Without quoting the rule, explain why you cannot accede to the request and suggest alternative sources
    C. Describe how carefully the request was considered before classifying it as subject to the rule forbidding the issuance of such information
    D. Acknowledge receipt of the letter and advise that the requested information is not released to the public

34.____

35. Suppose you assist in supervising a staff which has rather high morale, and your own supervisor asks you to poll the staff to find out who will be able to work overtime this particular evening to help complete emergency work.
Which of the following approaches would be MOST likely to win their cooperation while maintaining their morale?
    A. Tell them that the better assignments will be given only to those who work overtime
    B. Tell them that occasional overtime is a job requirement
    C. Assure them they'll be doing you a personal favor
    D. Let them know clearly why the overtime is needed

36. Suppose that you have been asked to write and to prepare for reproduction new departmental vacation leave regulations.
After you have written the new regulations, all of which fit on one page, which one of the following would be the BESST method of reproducing 1,000 copies?
    A. An outside private printer, because you can best maintain confidentiality using this technique
    B. Xeroxing, because the copies will have the best possible appearance
    C. Typing copies, because you will be certain that there are the fewest possible errors
    D. Including it in the next company newsletter

37. Administration is the center, but not necessarily the source, of all ideas for procedural improvement.
The MOST significant implication that this principle bears for the administrative officer is that
    A. before procedural improvements are introduced, they should be approved by a majority of the staff
    B. it is the unique function of the administrative officer to derive and introduce procedural improvements
    C. the administrative officer should derive ideas and suggestions for procedural improvement from all possible sources, introducing any that promise to be effective
    D. the administrative officer should view employee grievances as the chief source of procedural improvements

38. Your bureau is assigned an important task.
Of the following, the function that you, as an administrative officer, can LEAST reasonably be expected to perform under these circumstances is
    A. division of the large job into individual tasks
    B. establishment of *production lines* within the bureau
    C. performance personally of a substantial share of all the work
    D. check up to see that the work has been done well

39. Suppose that you have broken a complex job into its smaller components before making assignments to the employees under your jurisdiction.
Of the following, the LEAST advisable procedure to follow from that point is to
   A. give each employee a picture of the importance of his work for the success of the total job
   B. establish a definite line of work flow and responsibility
   C. post a written memorandum of the best method for performing each job
   D. teach a number of alternative methods for doing each job

40. As an administrative officer, you are requested to draw up an organization chart of the whole department.
Of the following, the MOST important characteristic of such a chart is that it will
   A. include all peculiarities and details of the organization which distinguish it from any other
   B. be a schematic representation of purely administrative functions within the department
   C. present a modification of the actual departmental organization in the light of principles of scientific management
   D. present an accurate picture of the lines of authority and responsibility

KEY (CORRECT ANSWERS)

1.	A	11.	B	21.	A	31.	B
2.	C	12.	D	22.	B	32.	C
3.	C	13.	C	23.	A	33.	C
4.	D	14.	B	24.	C	34.	A
5.	D	15.	D	25.	B	35.	D
6.	C	16.	A	26.	C	36.	B
7.	D	17.	C	27.	B	37.	C
8.	B	18.	A	28.	C	38.	C
9.	C	19.	C	29.	D	39.	D
10.	C	20.	A	30.	D	40.	D

TEST 2

DIRECTIONS: Each question or incomplete statement is followed by several suggested answers or completions. Select the one that BEST answers the question or completes the statement. *PRINT THE LETTER OF THE CORRECT ANSWER IN THE SPACE AT THE RIGHT.*

Questions 1-10.

DIRECTIONS: In each of Questions 1 through 10, a pair of related words written in capital letters is followed by four other pairs of words. For each question, select the pair of words which MOST closely expresses a relationship similar to that of the pair in capital letters.

    SAMPLE QUESTION:
       BOAT – DOCK

    A. air plane – hangar   B. rain – snow
    C. cloth – cotton   D. hunger - food

Choice A is the answer to this sample question since, of the choices given, the relationship between airplane and hangar is most similar to the relationship between boat and dock.

1. AUTOMOBILE – FACTORY
   A. tea – lemon   B. wheel – engine
   C. pot – flower   D. paper – mill

2. GIRDER – BRIDGE
   A. petal – flower   B. street – sidewalk
   C. meat – vegetable   D. sun – storm

3. RADIUS – CIRCLE
   A. brick – building   B. tie – tracks
   C. spoke – wheel   D. axle – tire

4. DISEASE – RESEARCH
   A. death – poverty   B. speech – audience
   C. problem – conference   D. invalid – justice

5. CONCLUSION – INTRODUCTION
   A. commencement – beginning   B. housing – motor
   C. caboose – engine   D. train – cabin

6. SOCIETY – LAW
   A. baseball – rules   B. jury – law
   C. cell – prisoner   D. sentence – jury

7. PLAN – ACCOMPLISHMENT 7.____
   A. deed – fact
   B. method – success
   C. graph – chart
   D. rules – manual

8. ORDER – GOVERNMENT 8.____
   A. chaos – administration
   B. confusion – pandemonium
   C. rule – stability
   D. despair – hope

9. TYRANNY – FREEDOM 9.____
   A. despot – mob
   B. wealth – poverty
   C. nobility – commoners
   D. dictatorship – democracy

10. FAX – LETTER 10.____
    A. hare – tortoise
    B. lie – truth
    C. number – word
    D. report – research

Questions 11-16.

DIRECTIONS: Questions 11 through 16 are to be answered SOLELY on the basis of the information given in the passage below.

Inherent in all organized endeavors is the need to resolve the individual differences involved in conflict. Conflict may be either a positive or negative factor, since it may lead to creativity, innovation, and progress, on the one hand, or it may result, on the other hand, in a deterioration or even destruction of the organization. Thus, some forms of conflict are desirable, whereas others are undesirable and ethically wrong.

There are three management strategies which deal with interpersonal conflict. In the "divide-and-rule strategy," management attempts to maintain control by limiting the conflict to those directly involved and preventing their disagreement from spreading to the larger group. The "suppression –of-differences strategy" entails ignoring conflicts or pretending they are irrelevant. In the "working-through-differences strategy," management actively attempts to solve or resolve intergroup or interpersonal conflicts. Of the three strategies, only the last directly attacks and has the potential for eliminating the causes of conflict. An essential part of this strategy, however, is its employment by a committed and relatively mature management team.

11. According to the above passage, the *divide-and-rule strategy* for dealing with 11.____
    conflict is the attempt to
    A. involve other people in the conflict
    B. restrict the conflict to those participating in it
    C. divide the conflict into positive and negative factors
    D. divide the conflict into a number of smaller ones

12. The word *conflict* is used in relation to both positive and negative factors in this 12.____
    passage.
    Which one of the following words is MOST likely to describe the activity which the word *conflict*, in the sense of the passage, implies?
    A. Competition   B. Cooperation   C. Confusion   D. Aggression

13. According to the above passage, which one of the following characteristics is shared by both the *suppression-of-difference strategy* and the *divide-and-rule strategy*?   13.____
    A. Pretending that conflicts are irrelevant
    B. Preventing conflicts from spreading to the group situation
    C. Failure to directly attack the causes of conflict
    D. Actively attempting to resolve interpersonal conflict

14. According to the above passage, the successful resolution of interpersonal conflict requires   14.____
    A. allowing the group to mediate conflicts between two individuals
    B. division of the conflict into positive and negative factors
    C. involvement of a committed, mature management team
    D. ignoring minor conflicts until they threaten the organization

15. Which can be MOST reasonably inferred from the above passage? A conflict between two individuals is LEAST likely to continue when management uses   15.____
    A. the *working-through-differences strategy*
    B. the *suppression-of-differences strategy*
    C. the *divide-and-rule strategy*
    D. a combination of all three strategies

16. According to the above passage, a DESIRABLE result of conflict in an organization is when conflict   16.____
    A. exposes production problems in the organization
    B. can be easily ignored by management
    C. results in advancement of more efficient managers
    D. leads to development of new methods

Questions 17-23.

DIRECTIONS: Questions 17 through 23 are to be answered SOLELY on the basis of the information given in the passage below.

Modern management places great emphasis on the concept of communication. The communication process consists of the steps through which an idea or concept passes from its inception by one person, the sender, until it is acted upon by another person, the receiver. Through an understanding of these steps and some of the possible barriers that may occur, more effective communication may be achieved. The first step in the communication process is ideation by the sender. This is the formation of the intended content of the message he wants to transmit. In the next step, encoding, the sender organizes his ideas into a series of symbols designed to communicate his message to his intended receiver. He selects suitable words or phrases that can be understood by the receiver, and he also selects the appropriate media to be used—for example, memorandum, conference, etc. The third step is transmission of the encoded message through selected channels in the organizational structure. In the fourth step, the receiver enters the process by tuning in to receive the message. If the receiver does not function, however, the message is lost. For example, if the message is oral, the receiver must be a good listener. The fifth step is decoding of the message by the receiver, as for example, by changing words into ideas. At this step, the decoded message may not be the same idea that the sender originally encoded because the sender and receiver have different perceptions regarding the meaning of certain words.

Finally, the receiver acts or responds. He may file the information, ask for more information, or take other action. There can be no assurance, however, that communication has taken place unless there is some type of feedback to the sender in the form of an acknowledgement that the message was received.

17. According to the above passage, *ideation* is the process by which the
    A. sender develops the intended content of the message
    B. sender organizes his ideas into a series of symbols
    C. receiver tunes in to receive the message
    D. receiver decodes the message

18. In the last sentence of the passage, the word *feedback* refers to the process by which the sender is assured that the
    A. receiver filed the information
    B. receiver's perception is the same as his own
    C. message was received
    D. message was poorly interpreted

19. Which one of the following BEST shows the order of the steps in the communication process as described in the passage?
    A. 1 – ideation   2 – encoding
       3 – decoding   4 – transmission
       5 – receiving   6 – action
       7 – feedback to the sender
    B. 1 – ideation   2 – encoding
       3 – transmission   4 – decoding
       5 – receiving   6 – action
       7 – feedback to the sender
    C. 1 – ideation   2 – decoding
       3 – transmission   4 – receiving
       5 – encoding   6 – action
       7 – feedback to the sender
    D. 1 – ideation   2 – encoding
       3 – transmission   4 – receiving
       5 – decoding   6 – action
       7 – feedback to the sender

20. Which one of the following BEST expresses the main theme of the passage?
    A. Different individuals have the same perceptions regarding the meaning of words.
    B. An understanding of the steps in the communication process may achieve better communication.
    C. Receivers play a passive role in the communication process.
    D. Senders should not communicate with receivers who transmit feedback.

21. The above passage implies that a receiver does NOT function properly when he
    A. transmits feedback
    B. files the information
    C. is a poor listener
    D. asks for more information

    21._____

22. Which of the following, according to the above passage, is included in the SECOND step of the communication process?
    A. Selecting the appropriate media to be used in transmission
    B. Formulation of the intended content of the message
    C. Using appropriate media to respond to the receiver's feedback
    D. Transmitting the message through selected channels in the organization

    22._____

23. The above passage implies that the *decoding* process is MOST NEARLY the reverse of the _____ process.
    A. transmission   B. receiving   C. feedback   D. encoding

    23._____

Questions 24-27.

DIRECTIONS: Questions 24 through 27 are to be answered SOLELY on the basis of the information given in the passage below.

A personnel researcher has at his disposal various approaches for obtaining information, analyzing it, and arriving at conclusions that have value in predicting and affecting the behavior of people at work. The type of method to be used depends on such factors as the nature of the research problem, the available data, and the attitude of those people being studied to the various kinds of approaches. While the experimental approach, with its use of control groups, is the most refined type of study, there are others that are often found useful in personnel research. Surveys, in which the researcher obtains facts on a problem from a variety of sources, are employed in research on wages, fringe benefits, and labor relations. Historical studies are used to trace the development of problems in order to understand them better and to isolate possible causative factors. Case studies are generally developed to explore all the details of a particular problem that is representative of other similar problems. A researcher chooses the most appropriate form of study for the problem he is investigating. He should recognize, however, that the experimental method, commonly referred to as the scientific method, if used validly and reliably, gives the most conclusive results.

24. The above statement discusses several approaches used to obtain information on particular problems.
    Which of the following may be MOST reasonably concluded from the passage? A(n)
    A. historical study cannot determine causative factors
    B. survey is often used in research on fringe benefits
    C. case study is usually used to explore a problem that is unique and unrelated to other problems
    D. experimental study is used when the scientific approach to a problem fails

    24._____

25. According to the above passage, all of the following are factors that may determine the type of approach a researcher uses EXCEPT
    A. the attitudes of people toward being used in control groups
    B. the number of available sources
    C. his desire to isolate possible causative factors
    D. the degree of accuracy he requires

26. The words *scientific method*, used in the last sentence of the paragraph, refer to a type of study which, according to the paragraph,
    A. uses a variety of sources
    B. traces the development of problems
    C. uses control group
    D. analyzes the details of a representative problem

27. Which of the following can be MOST reasonably concluded from the above passage?
    In obtaining and analyzing information on a particular problem, a researcher employs the method which is the
    A. most accurate
    B. most suitable
    C. least expensive
    D. least time-consuming

Questions 28-31.

DIRECTIONS: Questions 28 through 31 are to be answered according to the information given in the following graph, which indicates at 5-year intervals the number of citations issued for various offenses from the year 2000 to the year 2020.

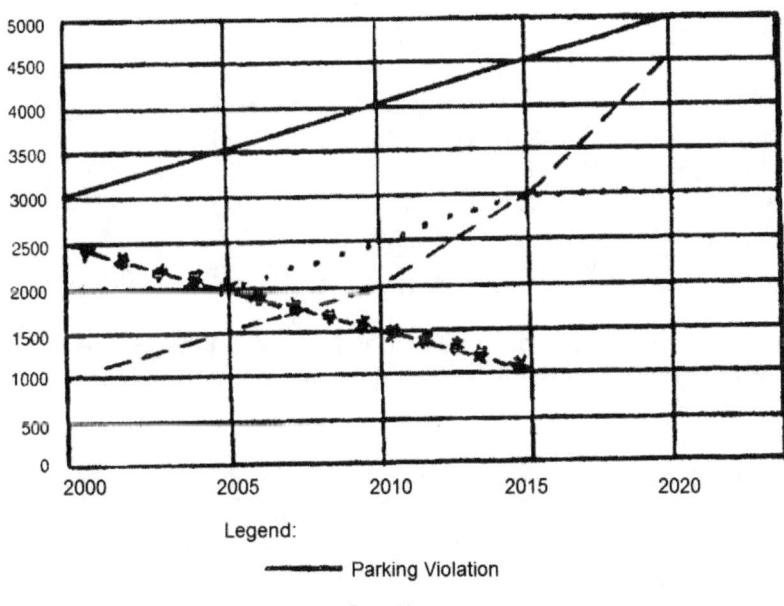

Legend:
——— Parking Violation
— — — Drug Use
· · · · Dangerous Weapons
✶–✶–✶–✶ Improper Dress

28. Over the 20-year period, which offense shows an AVERAGE rate of increase of more than 150 citations per year?
    A. Parking Violations
    B. Dangerous Weapons
    C. Drug Use
    D. None of the above

28.____

29. Over the 20-year period, which offense shows a CONSTANT rate of increase or decrease?
    A. Parking Violations
    B. Drug Use
    C. Dangerous Weapons
    D. Improper Dress

29.____

30. Which offense shows a TOTAL INCREASE OR DECREASE of 50% for the full 20-year period?
    A. Parking Violations
    B. Drug Use
    C. Dangerous Weapons
    D. Improper Dress

30.____

31. The percentage increase in total citations issued from 2005 to 2010 is MOST NEARLY
    A. 7%
    B. 11%
    C. 21%
    D. 41%

31.____

Questions 32-35.

DIRECTIONS: Questions 32 through 35 are to be answered SOLELY on the basis of the information given in the following chart, which shows the annual number of administrative actions completed for the four divisions of a bureau. Assume that the figures remain stable from year to year.

Administrative Actions	DIVISIONS				TOTALS
	W	X	Y	Z	
Telephone Inquiries Answered	8,000	6,800	7,500	4,800	27,100
Interviews Conducted	500	630	550	500	2,180
Applications Processed	15,000	18,000	14,500	9,500	57,000
Letters Typed	2,500	4,400	4,350	3,250	14,500
Reports Completed	200	250	100	50	600
Totals	26,200	30,080	27,000	18,100	101,380

32. In which division is the number of Applications Processed the GREATEST percentage of the total Administrative Action for that division?
    A. W
    B. X
    C. Y
    D. Z

32.____

33. The bureau chief is considering a plant that would consolidate the typing of letters in a separate unit. This unit would be responsible for the typing of letters for all divisions in which the number of letters typed exceeds 15% of the total number of Administrative Actions.
Under this plan, which of the following divisions would CONTINUE to type its own letters?
    A. W and X
    B. W, X, and Y
    C. X and Y
    D. X and Z

33.____

34. The setting up of a central information service that would be capable of answering 25% of the whole bureau's telephone inquiries is under consideration. Under such a plan, the divisions would gain for other activities that time previously spent on telephone inquiries.
Approximately how much total time would such a service gain for all four divisions if it requires 5 minutes to answer the average telephone inquiry? _____ hours.
   A. 500   B. 515   C. 565   D. 585

34._____

35. Assume that the rate of production shown in the table can be projected as accurate for the coming year and that monthly output is constant for each type of administrative action within a division. Division Y is scheduled to work exclusively on a 4-month long special project during that year. During the period of the project, Division Y's regular workload will be divided evenly among the remaining divisions.
Using the figures in the table, what would be MOST NEARLY the percentage increase in the total Administrative Actions completed by Division Z for the year?
   A. 8%   B. 16%   C. 25%   D. 50%

35._____

36. You have conducted a traffic survey a 10 two-lane bridges and find the traffic between 4:30 and 5:30 P.M. average 665 cars per bridge that hour. You can't find the tabulation sheet for Bridge #7, but you know that 6066 cars were counted at the other 9 bridges.
Determine from this how many must have been counted at Bridge #7.
   A. 584   B. 674   C. 665   D. 607

36._____

37. You pay temporary help $11.20 per hour and regular employees $12.00 per hour. Your workload is temporarily heavy, so you need 20 hours of extra regular employees' time to catch up. If you do this on overtime, you must pay time-and-a-half. If you use temporary help, it takes 25% more time to do the job.
What is the difference in cost between the two alternatives?
   A. $20 more for temporary   B. $40 more for temporary
   C. $80 more for regular   D. $136 more for regular

37._____

38. An experienced clerk can process the mailing of annual forms in 9 day. A new clerk takes 14 days to process them.
If they work together, how many days MOST NEARLY will it take to do the processing?
   A. 4½   B. 5½   C. 6½   D. 7

38._____

39. A certain administrative aide is usually able to successfully handle 27% of all telephone inquiries without assistance. In a particular month, he receives 1,200 inquiries and handles 340 of them successfully on his own.
How many more inquiries has he handled successfully in that month than would have been expected of him based on his usual rate?
   A. 10   B. 16   C. 24   D. 44

39._____

40. Suppose that on a scaled drawing of an office building floor, ½ inch represents three feet of actual floor dimensions.
A floor which is, in fact, 75 feet wide and 132 feet long has which of the following dimensions on this scaled drawing? _____ inches wide and _____ inches long.
   A. 9.5; 20.5   B. 12.5; 22   C. 17;32   D. 25; 44

40._____

41. In a division of clerks and stenographers, 15 people are currently employed, 20% of whom are stenographers.
If management plans are to maintain the current number of stenographers, but to increase the clerical staff to the point where 12% of the total staff are stenographers, what is the MAXIMUM number of additional clerks that should be hired to meet these plans?
   A. 3   B. 8   C. 10   D. 12

41._____

42. Suppose that a certain agency had a 2018 budget of $1,200,500. The 2019 budget was 7% higher than that of 2018, and the 2020 budget was 8% higher than that of 2019.
Of the following, which one is MOST NEARLY that agency's budget for 2020?
   A. $1,177,624   B. $1,261,737   C. $1,265,575   D. $1,271,738

42._____

Questions 43-50.

DIRECTIONS: Your office keeps a file card record of the work assignments for all the employees in a certain bureau. On each card is the employee's name, a work assignment code number, and the date of this assignment. In this filing system, the employee's name is filed alphabetically, the work assignment code is filed numerically, and the date of assignment is filed chronologically (earliest date first).

Each of Questions 43 through 50 represents five cards to be filed, numbered (1) through (5) shown in Column I. Each card is made up of the employee's name, a work assignment code number shown in parentheses, and the date of this assignment. The cards are to be filed according to the following rules:

First: File in alphabetical order.
Second: When two or more cards have the same employee's name, file according to the work assignment number, beginning with the lowest number.
Third: When two or more cards have the same employee's name and same assignment number, file according to the assignment date beginning with earliest date.

Column II shows the cards arranged in four different orders. Pick the answer (A, B, C, or D) in Column II which shows the cards arranged correctly according to the above filing rules.

SAMPLE QUESTION:
                    Column I   Column II
    (1)   Cluney   (486503)   6/17/07   A. 2, 3, 4, 1, 5
    (2)   Roster   (246611)   5/10/06   B. 2, 5, 1, 3, 4
    (3)   Altool   (711433)   10/15/07   C. 3, 2, 1, 4, 5
    (4)   Cluney   (527610)   12/18/06   D. 3, 5, 1, 4, 2
    (5)   Cluney   (486500)   4/8/07

The CORRECT way to file the cards is:
    (3)   Altool   (711433)   10/15/07
    (5)   Cluney   (486500)   4/8/07
    (1)   Cluney   (486503)   6/17/07
    (4)   Cluney   (527610)   12/18/06
    (2)   Roster   (246611)   5/10/06

The correct filing order is shown by the numbers in front of each name (3, 5, 1, 4, 2). The answer to the sample question is the letter in Column II in front of the numbers 3, 5, 1, 4, 2. This answer is D.

			Column I		Column II	
43.	(1)	Prichard	(013469)	4/6/06	A. 5, 4, 3, 2, 1	43.___
	(2)	Parks	(678941)	2/7/06	B. 1, 2, 5, 3, 4	
	(3)	Williams	(551467)	3/6/05	C. 2, 1, 5, 3, 4	
	(4)	Wilson	(551466)	8/9/02	D. 1, 5, 4, 3, 2	
	(5)	Stanhope	(300014)	8/9/02		
44.	(1)	Ridgeway	(623809)	8/11/06	A. 5, 1, 3, 4, 2	44.___
	(2)	Travers	(305439)	4/5/02	B. 5, 1, 3, 2, 4	
	(3)	Tayler	(818134)	7/5/03	C. 1, 5, 3, 2, 4	
	(4)	Travers	(305349)	5/6/05	D. 1, 5, 4, 2, 3	
	(5)	Ridgeway	(62309)	10/9/06		
45.	(1)	Jaffe	(384737)	2/19/06	A. 3, 5, 2, 4, 1	45.___
	(2)	Inez	(859176)	8/8/07	B. 3, 5, 2, 1, 4	
	(3)	Ingrahm	(946460)	8/6/04	C. 2, 3, 5, 1, 4	
	(4)	Karp	(256146)	5/5/05	D. 2, 3, 5, 4, 1	
	(5)	Ingrahm	(946460)	6/4/05		
46.	(1)	Marrano	(369421)	7/24/04	A. 1, 5, 3, 4, 2	46.___
	(2)	Marks	(652910)	2/23/06	B. 3, 5, 4, 2, 1	
	(3)	Netto	(556772)	3/10/07	C. 2, 4, 1, 5, 3	
	(4)	Marks	(652901)	2/17/07	D. 4, 2, 1, 5, 3	
	(5)	Netto	(556772)	6/17/05		
47.	(1)	Abernathy	(712467)	6/23/05	A. 5, 3, 1, 2, 4	47.___
	(2)	Acevedo	(680262)	6/23/03	B. 5, 4, 2, 3, 1	
	(3)	Aaron	(967647)	1/17/04	C. 1, 3, 5, 2, 4	
	(4)	Acevedo	(680622)	5/14/02	D. 2, 4, 1, 5, 3	
	(5)	Aaron	(967647)	4/1/00		

48. (1) Simon   (645219) 8/19/05   A. 4, 1, 2, 5, 3
    (2) Simon   (645219) 9/2/03   B. 4, 5, 2, 1, 3
    (3) Simons   (645218) 7/7/05   C. 3, 5, 2, 1, 4
    (4) Simms   (646439) 10/12/06   D. 5, 1, 2, 3, 4
    (5) Simon   (645219) 10/16/02

49. (1) Rappaport (312230) 6/11/06   A. 4, 3, 1, 2, 5
    (2) Rascio   (777510) 2/9/05   B. 4, 3, 1, 5, 2
    (3) Rappaport (312230) 7/3/02   C. 3, 4, 1, 5, 2
    (4) Rapaport (312330) 9/6/05   D. 5, 2, 4, 3, 1
    (5) Rascio   (777501) 7/7/05

50. (1) Johnson   (843250) 6/8/02   A. 1, 3, 2, 4, 5
    (2) Johnson   (843205) 4/3/05   B. 1, 3, 2, 5, 4
    (3) Johnson   (843205) 8/6/02   C. 3, 2, 1, 4, 5
    (4) Johnson   (843602) 3/8/06   D. 3, 2, 1, 5, 4
    (5) Johnson   (843602) 8/3/05

KEY (CORRECT ANSWERS)

1. D	11. B	21. C	31. B	41. C
2. A	12. A	22. A	32. B	42. D
3. C	13. C	23. D	33. A	43. C
4. C	14. C	24. B	34. C	44. A
5. C	15. A	25. D	35. B	45. C
6. A	16. D	26. C	36. A	46. D
7. B	17. A	27. B	37. C	47. A
8. C	18. C	28. C	38. B	48. B
9. D	19. D	29. A	39. B	49. B
10. A	20. B	30. C	40. B	50. D

READING COMPREHENSION
UNDERSTANDING AND INTERPRETING WRITTEN MATERIAL
EXAMINATION SECTION
TEST 1

DIRECTIONS: Each question or incomplete statement is followed by several suggested answers or completions. Select the one that BEST answers the question or completes the statement. *PRINT THE LETTER OF THE CORRECT ANSWER IN THE SPACE AT THE RIGHT.*

Questions 1-5.

DIRECTIONS: Questions 1 through 5 are to be answered SOLELY on the basis of the following passage.

The most effective control mechanism to prevent gross incompetence on the part of public employees is a good personnel program. The personnel officer in the line departments and the central personnel agency should exert positive leadership to raise levels of performance. Although the key factor is the quality of the personnel recruited, staff members other than personnel officers can make important contributions to efficiency. Administrative analysts, now employed in many agencies, make detailed studies of organization and procedures, with the purpose of eliminating delays, waste, and other inefficiencies. Efficiency is, however, more than a question of good organization and procedures; it is also the product of the attitudes and value of the public employees. Personal motivation can provide the will to be efficient. The best management studies will not result in substantial improvement of the performance of those employees who feel no great urge to wok up to their abilities.

1. The above passage indicates that the KEY factor in preventing gross incompetence of public employees is the
    A. hiring of administrative analysts to assist personnel people
    B. utilization of effective management studies
    C. overlapping of responsibility
    D. quality of the employees hired

1.____

2. According to the above passage, the central personnel agency staff SHOULD
    A. work more closely with administrative analysts in the line departments than with personnel officers
    B. make a serious effort to avoid jurisdictional conflicts with personnel officers in line departments
    C. contribute to improving the quality of work of public employees
    D. engage in a comprehensive program to change the public's negative image of public employees

2.____

3. The above passage indicates that efficiency in an organization can BEST be 3.____
brought about by
   A. eliminating ineffective control mechanisms
   B. instituting sound organizational procedures
   C. promoting competent personnel
   D. recruiting people with desire to do good work

4. According to the above passage, the purpose of administrative analysts 4.____
in a public agency is to
   A. prevent injustice to the public employee
   B. promote the efficiency of the agency
   C. protect the interests of the public
   D. ensure the observance of procedural due process

5. The above passage implies that a considerable rise in the quality of work of 5.____
public employees can be brought about by
   A. encouraging positive employee attitudes toward work
   B. controlling personnel officers who exceed their powers
   C. creating warm personal associations among public employees in an agency
   D. closing loopholes in personnel organization and procedures

Questions 6-8.

DIRECTIONS: Questions 6 through 8 are to be answered SOLELY on the basis of the following passage.

EMPLOYEE NEEDS

The greatest waste in industry and in government may be that of human resources. This waste usually derives not from employees' unwillingness or inability, but from management's ineptness to meet the maintenance and motivational needs of employees. Maintenance needs refer to such needs as providing employees with safe places to work, written work rules, job security, adequate salary, employer-sponsored social activities, and with knowledge of their role in the overall framework of the organization. However, of greatest significance to employees are the motivational needs of job growth, achievement, responsibility, and recognition.

Although employee dissatisfaction may stem from either poor maintenance or poor motivation factors, the outward manifestation of the dissatisfaction may be very much like, i.e., negativism, complaints, deterioration of performance, and so forth. The improvement in the lighting of an employee's work area or raising his level of ay won't do much good if the source of the dissatisfaction is the absence of a meaningful assignment. By the same token, if an employee is dissatisfied with what he considers inequitable pay, the introduction of additional challenge in his work may simply make matters worse.

It is relatively easy for an employee to express frustration by complaining about pay, washroom conditions, fringe benefits, and so forth; but most people cannot easily express resentment in terms of the more abstract concepts concerning job growth, responsibility, and achievement.

It would be wrong to assume that there is no interaction between maintenance and motivational needs of employee. For example, conditions of high motivation often overshadow poor maintenance conditions. If an organization is in a period of strong growth and expansion, opportunities for job growth, responsibility, recognition, and achievement are usually abundant, but the rapid growth may have outrun the upkeep of maintenance factors. In this situation, motivation may be high, but only if employees recognize the poor maintenance conditions as unavoidable and temporary. The subordination of maintenance factors cannot go on indefinitely, even with the highest motivation.

Both maintenance and motivation factors influence the behavior of all employees, but employees are not identical and, furthermore, the needs of any individual do not remain orientation toward maintenance factors and those with greater sensitivity toward motivation factors.

A highly maintenance-oriented individual, preoccupied with the factors peripheral to his job rather than the job itself, is more concerned with comfort than challenge. He does not get deeply involved with his work but does with the condition of his work area, toilet facilities, and his time for going to lunch. By contrast, a strongly motivation-oriented employee is usually relatively indifferent to his surroundings and is caught up in the pursuit of work goals.

Fortunately, there are few people who are either exclusively maintenance-oriented or purely motivation-oriented. The former would be deadwood in an organization, while the latter might trample on those around him in his pursuit to achieve his goals.

6. With respect to employee motivational and maintenance needs, the management policies of an organization which is growing rapidly will probably result
    A. more in meeting motivational needs rather than maintenance needs
    B. more in meeting maintenance needs rather than motivational needs
    C. in meeting both of these needs equally
    D. in increased effort to define the motivational and maintenance needs of its employees

7. In accordance with the above passage, which of the following CANNOT be considered as an example of an employee maintenance need for railroad clerks?
    A. Providing more relief periods
    B. Providing fair salary increases at periodic intervals
    C. Increasing job responsibilities
    D. Increasing health insurance benefits

8. Most employees in an organization may be categorized as being interested in
    A. maintenance needs only
    B. motivational needs only
    C. both motivational and maintenance needs
    D. money only, to the exclusion of all other needs

Questions 9-11.

DIRECTIONS: Questions 9 through 11 are to be answered SOLELY on the basis of the following passage.

GOOD EMPLOYEE PRACTICES

As a city employee, you will be expected to take an interest in you work and perform the duties of your job to the best of your ability and in a spirit of cooperation. Nothing shows an interest in your work more than coming to work on time, not only at the start of the day but also when returning from lunch. If it is necessary for you to keep a personal appointment at lunch hour which might cause a delay in getting back to work on time, you should explain the situation to your supervisor and get his approval to come back a little late before you leave for lunch.

You should do everything that is asked of you willingly and consider important even the small jobs that your supervisor gives you. Although these jobs may seem unimportant, if you forget to do them or if you don't do them right, trouble may develop later.

Getting along well with your fellow workers will add much to the enjoyment of your work. You should respect your fellow workers and try to see their side when a disagreement arises. The better you get along with your fellow workers and your supervisor, the better you will like your job and the better you will be able to do it.

9. According to the above passage, in your job as a city employee, you are expected to
   A. show a willingness to cooperate on the job
   B. get your supervisor's approval before keeping any personal appointments at lunch hour
   C. avoid doing small jobs that seem unimportant
   D. do the easier jobs at the start of the day and the more difficult ones later on

10. According to the above passage, getting to work on time shows that you
    A. need the job
    B. have an interest in your work
    C. get along well with your fellow workers
    D. like your supervisor

11. According to the above passage, the one of the following statements that is NOT true is:
    A. If you do a small job wrong, trouble may develop
    B. You should respect your fellow workers
    C. If you disagree with a fellow worker, you should try to see his side of the story
    D. The less you get along with your supervisor, the better you will be able to do your job

Questions 12-15.

DIRECTIONS: Questions 12 through 15 are to be answered SOLELY on the basis of the following passage.

EMPLOYEE SUGGESTIONS

To increase the effectiveness of the city government, the city asks its employees to offer suggestions when they feel an improvement could be made in some government operation. The Employees' Suggestions Program was started to encourage city employees to do this. Through this Program, which is only for city employees, cash awards may be given to those whose suggestions are submitted and approved. Suggestions are looked for not only from supervisors but from all city employees as any city employee may get an idea which might be approved and contribute greatly to the solution of some problem of city government.

Therefore, all suggestions for improvement are welcome, whether they be suggestions on how to improve working conditions, or on how to increase the speed with which work is done, or on how to reduce or eliminate such things as waste, time losses, accidents or fire hazards. There are, however, a few types of suggestions for which cash awards cannot be given. An example of this type would be a suggestion to increase salaries or a suggestion to change the regulations about annual leave or about sick leave. The number of suggestions sent in has increased sharply during the past few years. It is hoped that it will keep increasing in the future in order to meet the city's needs for more ideas for improved ways of doing things.

12. According to the above passage, the MAIN reason why the city asks its employees for suggestions about government operations is to
    A. increase the effectiveness of the city government
    B. show that the Employees' Suggestion Program is working well
    C. show that everybody helps run the city government
    D. have the employee win a prize

13. According to the above passage, the Employees' Suggestion Program can approve awards ONLY for those suggestions that come from
    A. city employees
    B. city employees who are supervisors
    C. city employees who are not supervisors
    D. experienced employee of the city

14. According to the above passage, a cash award cannot be given through the Employees' Suggestion Program for a suggestion about
    A. getting work done faster
    B. helping prevent accidents on the job
    C. increasing the amount of annual leave for city employees
    D. reducing the chance of fire where city employees work

15. According to the above passage, the suggestions sent in during the past few years have
    A. all been approved
    B. generally been well written
    C. been mostly about reducing or eliminating waste
    D. been greater in number than before

Questions 16-18.

DIRECTIONS: Questions 16 through 18 are to be answered SOLELY on the basis of the following passage.

The supervisor will gain the respect of the members of his staff and increase his influence over them by controlling his temper and avoiding criticizing anyone publicly. When a mistake is made, the good supervisor will take it over with the employee quietly and privately. The supervisor will listen to the employee's story, suggest the better way of doing the job, and offer help so the mistake won't happen again. Before closing the discussion, the supervisor should try to find something good to say about other parts of the employee's work. Some praise and appreciation, along with instruction, is more likely to encourage an employee to improve in those areas where he is weakest.

16. A good title that would show the meaning of the above passage would be
    A. How to Correct Employee Errors
    B. How to Praise Employees
    C. Mistakes are Preventable
    D. The Weak Employee

17. According to the above passage, the work of an employee who has made a mistake is more likely to improve if the supervisor
    A. avoids criticizing him
    B. gives him a chance to suggest a better way of doing the work
    C. listens to the employee's excuses to see if he is right
    D. praises good work at the same time he corrects the mistake

18. According to the above passage, when a supervisor needs to correct an employee's mistake, it is important that he
    A. allow some time to go by after the mistake is made
    B. do so when other employee are not present
    C. show his influence with his tone of voice
    D. tell other employee to avoid the same mistake

Questions 19-23.

DIRECTIONS: Questions 19 through 23 are to be answered SOLELY on the basis of the following passage.

In studying the relationships of people to the organizational structure, it is absolutely necessary to identify and recognize the informal organizational structure. These relationships are necessary when coordination of a plan is attempted. They may be with *the boss*, line supervisors, staff personnel, or other representatives of the formal organization's hierarchy, and they may include the *liaison men* who serve as the leaders of the informal organization. An acquaintanceship with the people serving in these roles in the organization, and its formal counterpart, permits a supervisor to recognize sensitive areas in which it is simple to get conflict reaction. Avoidance of such areas, plus conscious efforts to inform other people of his own objectives for various plans, will usually enlist their aid and support. Planning *without* people can lead to disaster because the individuals who must act together to make any plan a success are more important than the plans themselves.

19. Of the following titles, the one that MOST clearly describes the above passage is
    A. Coordination of a Function
    B. Avoidance of Conflict
    C. Planning With People
    D. Planning Objectives

20. According to the above passage, attempts at coordinating plans may fail unless
    A. the plan's objectives are clearly set forth
    B. conflict between groups is resolved
    C. the plans themselves are worthwhile
    D. informal relationships are recognized

21. According to the above passage, conflict
    A. may, in some cases, be desirable to secure results
    B. produces more heat than light
    C. should be avoided at all costs
    D. possibilities can be predicted by a sensitive supervisor

22. The above passage implies that
    A. informal relationships are more important than formal structure
    B. the weakness of a formal structure depends upon informal relationships
    C. liaison men are the key people to consult when taking formal and informal structures into account
    D. individuals in a group are at least as important as the plans for the group

23. The above passage suggests that
    A. some planning can be disastrous
    B. certain people in sensitive areas should be avoided
    C. the supervisor should discourage acquaintanceships in the organization
    D. organizational relationships should be consciously limited

Questions 24-25.

DIRECTIONS: Questions 24 and 25 are to be answered SOLELY on the basis of the following passage.

Good personnel relations of an organization depend upon mutual confidence, trust, and good will. The basis of confidence is understanding. Most troubles start with people who do not understand each other. When the organization's intentions or motives are misunderstood, or when reasons for actions, practices, or policies are misconstrued, complete cooperation from individuals is not forthcoming. If management expects full cooperation from employees, it has a responsibility of sharing with them the information which is the foundation of proper understanding, confidence, and trust. Personnel management has long since outgrown the days when it was the vogue to *treat them rough and tell them nothing.* Up-to-date personnel management provides all possible information about the activities, aims, and purposes of the organization. It seems altogether creditable that a desire should exist among employees for such information which the best-intentioned executive might think would not interest them and which the worst-intentioned would think was none of their business.

24. The above passage implies that one of the causes of the difficulty which an organization might have with its personnel relations is that its employees
   A. have not expressed interest in the activities, aims, and purposes of the organization
   B. do not believe in the good faith of the organization
   C. have not been able to give full cooperation to the organization
   D. do not recommend improvements in the practices and policies of the organization

25. According to the above passage, in order for an organization to have good personnel relations, it is NOT essential that
   A. employees have confidence in the organization
   B. the purposes of the organization be understood by the employees
   C. employees have a desire for information about the organization
   D. information about the organization be communicated to employees

KEY (CORRECT ANSWERS)

1.	D		11.	D
2.	C		12.	A
3.	D		13.	A
4.	B		14.	C
5.	A		15.	D
6.	A		16.	A
7.	C		17.	D
8.	C		18.	B
9.	A		19.	C
10.	B		20.	D

21.	D
22.	D
23.	A
24.	B
25.	C

TEST 2

DIRECTIONS: Each question or incomplete statement is followed by several suggested answers or completions. Select the one that BEST answers the question or completes the statement. *PRINT THE LETTER OF THE CORRECT ANSWER IN THE SPACE AT THE RIGHT.*

Questions 1-8.

DIRECTIONS: Questions 1 through 8 are to be answered SOLELY on the basis of the following passage.

Important figures in education and in public affairs have recommended development of a private organization sponsored in part by various private foundations which would offer installment payment plans to full-time matriculated students in accredited colleges and universities in the United States and Canada. Contracts would be drawn to cover either tuition and fees, or tuition, fees, room and board in college facilities, from one year up to and including six years. A special charge, which would vary with the length of the contract, would be added to the gross repayable amount. This would be in addition to interest at a rate which would vary with the income of the parents. There would be a 3% annual interest charge for families with total income, before income taxes, of $50,000 or less. The rate would increase by 1/10 of 1% for every $1,000 of additional net income in excess of $50,000 up to a maximum of 10% interest. Contracts would carry an insurance provision on the life of the parent or guardian who signs the contract; all contracts must have the signature of a parent or guardian. Payment would be scheduled in equal monthly installments.

1. Which of the following students would be eligible for the payment plan described in the above passage? A
   A. matriculated student taking six semester hours toward a graduate degree
   B. matriculated student taking seventeen semester hours toward an undergraduate degree
   C. graduate matriculated at the University of Mexico taking eighteen semester hours toward a graduate degree
   D. student taking eighteen semester hours in a special pre-matriculation program

1.____

2. According to the above passage, the organization described would be sponsored in part by
   A. private foundations
   B. colleges and universities
   C. persons in the field of education
   D. persons in public life

2.____

3. Which of the following expenses could NOT be covered by a contract with the organization described in the above passage?
   A. Tuition amounting to $20,000 per year
   B. Registration and laboratory fees
   C. Meals at restaurants near the college
   D. Rent for an apartment in a college dormitory

3.____

4. The total amount to be paid would include ONLY the
   A. principal
   B. principal and interest
   C. principal, interest, and special charge
   D. principal, interest, special charge, and fee

5. The contract would carry insurance on the
   A. life of the student
   B. life of the student's parents
   C. income of the parents of the student
   D. life of the parent who signed the contract

6. The interest rate for an annual loan of $25,000 from the organization described in the above passage for a student whose family's net income was $55,000 should be
   A. 3%   B. 3.5%   C. 4%   D. 4.5%

7. The interest rate for an annual loan of $35,000 from the organization described in the above passage for a student whose family's net income was $100,000 should be
   A. 5%   B. 8%   C. 9%   D. 10%

8. John Lee has submitted an application for the installment payment plan described in the above passage. John's mother and father have a store which grossed $500,000 last year, but the income which the family received from the store was $90,000 before taxes. They also had $5,000 income from stock dividends. They paid $10,000 in income taxes.
   The amount of income upon which the interest should be based is
   A. $85,000   B. $90,000   C. $95,000   D. $105,000

Questions 9-13.

DIRECTIONS: Questions 9 through 13 are to be answered SOLELY on the basis of the following passage.

Since the organization chart is pictorial in nature, there is a tendency for it to be drawn in an artistically balanced and appealing fashion, regardless of the realities of actual organizational structure. In addition to being subject to this distortion, there is the difficulty of communicating in any organization chart the relative importance or the relative size of various component parts of an organizational structure. Furthermore, because of the need for simplicity of design, an organization chart can never indicate the full extent of the interrelationships among the component parts of an organization.

These interrelationships are often just as vital as the specifications which an organization chart endeavors to indicate. Yet, if an organization chart were to be drawn with all the wide variety of criss-crossing communication and cooperation networks existent within a typical organization, the chart would probably be much more confusing than informative. It is also obvious that no organization chart as such can prove or disprove that the organizational structure it represents is effective in realizing the objectives of the organization. At best, an organization chart can only illustrate some of the various factors to be taken into consideration in understanding, devising, or altering organizational arrangements.

9. According to the above passage, an organization chart can be expected to portray the
    A. structure of the organization along somewhat ideal lines
    B. relative size of the organizational units quite accurately
    C. channels of information distribution within the organization graphically
    D. extent of the obligation of each unit to meet the organizational objectives

    9.____

10. According to the above passage, those aspects of internal functioning which are NOT shown on an organization chart
    A. can be considered to have little practical application in the operations of the organization
    B. might well be considered to be as important as the structural relationships which a chart does present
    C. could be the cause of considerable confusion in the operations of an organization which is quite large
    D. would be most likely to provide the information needed to determine the overall effectiveness of an organization

    10.____

11. In the above passage, the one of the following conditions which is NOT implied as being a defect of an organization chart is that an organization chart may
    A. present a picture of the organizational structure which is different from the structure that actually exists
    B. fail to indicate the comparative size of various organizational units
    C. be limited in its ability to convey some of the meaningful aspects of organizational relationships
    D. become less useful over a period of time during which the organizational facts which it illustrated have changed

    11.____

12. The one of the following which is the MOST suitable title for the above passage is
    A. The Design and Construction of an Organization Chart
    B. The Informal Aspects of an Organization Chart
    C. The Inherent Deficiencies of an Organization Chart
    D. The Utilization of a Typical Organization Chart

    12.____

13. It can be inferred from the above passage that the function of an organization chart is to
    A. contribute to the comprehension of the organization form and arrangements
    B. establish the capabilities of the organization to operate effectively
    C. provide a balanced picture of the operations of the organization
    D. eliminate the need for complexity in the organization's structure

    13.____

Questions 14-16.

DIRECTIONS: Questions 14 through 16 are to be answered SOLELY on the basis of the following passage.

In dealing with visitors to the school office, the school secretary must use initiative, tact, and good judgment. All visitors should be greeted promptly and courteously. The nature of their business should be determined quickly and handled expeditiously. Frequently, the secretary should be able to handle requests, deliveries, or passes herself. Her judgment should determine when a visitor should see members of the staff or the principal. Serious problems or doubtful cases should be referred to a supervisor.

14. In general, visitors should be handled by the
    A. school secretary
    B. principal
    C. appropriate supervisor
    D. person who is free

15. It is wise to obtain the following information from visitors:
    A. Name
    B. Nature of business
    C. Address
    D. Problems they have

16. All visitors who wish to see members of the staff should
    A. be permitted to do so
    B. produce identification
    C. do so for valid reasons only
    D. be processed by a supervisor

Questions 17-19.

DIRECTIONS: Questions 17 through 19 are to be answered SOLELY on the basis of the following passage.

Information regarding payroll status, salary differentials, promotional salary increments, deductions, and pension payments should be given to all members of the staff who have questions regarding these items. On occasion, if the secretary is uncertain regarding the information, the staff member should be referred to the principal or the appropriate agency. No question by a staff member regarding payroll status should be brushed aside as immaterial or irrelevant. The school secretary must always try to handle the question or pass it on to the person who can handle it.

17. If a teacher is dissatisfied with information regarding her salary status, as given by the school secretary, the matter should be
    A. dropped
    B. passed on to the principal
    C. passed on by the secretary to proper agency or the principal
    D. made a basis for grievance procedures

18. The following is an adequate summary of the above passage:
    A. The secretary must handle all payroll matters
    B. The secretary must handle all payroll matter or know who can handle them
    C. The secretary or the principal must handle all payroll matters
    D. Payroll matter too difficult to handle must be followed up until they are solved

19. The above passage implies that
    A. many teachers ask immaterial questions regarding payroll status
    B. few teachers ask irrelevant pension questions
    C. no teachers ask immaterial salary questions
    D. no question regarding salary should be considered irrelevant

Questions 20-22.

DIRECTIONS: Questions 20 through 22 are to be answered SOLELY on the basis of the following passage.

The necessity for good speech on the part of the school secretary cannot be overstated. The school secretary must deal with the general public, the pupils, the members of the staff, and the school supervisors. In every situation which involves the general public, the secretary serves as a representative of the school. In dealing with pupils, the secretary's speech must serve as a model from which students may guide themselves. Slang, colloquialisms, malapropisms, and local dialects must be avoided.

20. The above passage implies that the speech pattern of the secretary must be
    A. perfect
    B. very good
    C. average
    D. on a level with that of the pupils

21. The last sentence indicates that slang
    A. is acceptable
    B. occurs in all speech
    C. might be used occasionally
    D. should be shunned

22. The above passage implies that the speech of pupils
    A. may be influenced
    B. does not change readily
    C. is generally good
    D. is generally poor

Questions 23-25.

DIRECTIONS: Questions 23 through 25 are to be answered SOLELY on the basis of the following passage.

The school secretary who is engaged in the task of filing records and correspondence should follow a general set of rules. Items which are filed should be available to other secretaries or to supervisors quickly and easily by means of the application of a modicum of common sense and good judgment. Items which, by their nature, may be difficult to find should be cross-indexed. Folders and drawers should be neatly and accurately labeled. There should never be a large accumulation of papers which have not been filed.

23. A good general rule to follow in filing is that materials should be
    A. placed in folders quickly
    B. neatly stored
    C. readily available
    D. cross-indexed

24. Items that are filed should be available to
    A. the secretary charged with the task of filing
    B. secretaries and supervisors
    C. school personnel
    D. the principal

    24._____

25. A modicum of common sense means _____ common sense.
    A. an average amount of   B. a great deal of
    C. a little   D. no

    25._____

KEY (CORRECT ANSWERS)

1.	B		11.	D
2.	A		12.	C
3.	C		13.	A
4.	C		14.	A
5.	D		15.	B
6.	B		16.	C
7.	B		17.	C
8.	C		18.	B
9.	A		19.	D
10.	B		20.	B

21. D
22. A
23. C
24. B
25. C

TEST 3

DIRECTIONS: Each question or incomplete statement is followed by several suggested answers or completions. Select the one that BEST answers the question or completes the statement. *PRINT THE LETTER OF THE CORRECT ANSWER IN THE SPACE AT THE RIGHT.*

Questions 1-4.

DIRECTIONS: Questions 1 through 4 are to be answered SOLELY on the basis of the following passage.

    The proposition that administrative activity is essentially the same in all organizations appears to underlie some of the practices in the administration of private higher education. Although the practice is unusual in public education, there are numerous instances of industrial, governmental, or military administrators being assigned to private institutions of higher education and, to a lesser extent, of college and university presidents assuming administrative positions in other types of organizations. To test this theory that administrators are interchangeable, there is a need for systematic observation and classification. The myth that an educational administrator must first have experience in the teaching profession is firmly rooted in a long tradition that has historical prestige. The myth is bound up in the expectations of the public and personnel surrounding the administrator. Since administrative success depends significantly on how well an administrator meets the expectations others have of him, the myth may be more powerful than the special experience in helping the administrator attain organizational and educational objectives. Educational administrators who have risen through the teaching profession have often expressed nostalgia for the life of a teacher or scholar, but there is no evidence that this nostalgia contributes to administrative success.

1. Which of the following statements as completed is MOST consistent with the above passage?
   The greatest number of administrators has moved from
   A. industry and the military to government and universities
   B. government and universities to industry and the military
   C. government, the armed forces, and industry to colleges and universities
   D. colleges and universities to government, the armed forces, and industry

    1.____

2. Of the following, the MOST reasonable inference from the above passage is that a specific area requiring further research is the
   A. place of myth in the tradition and history of the educational profession
   B. relative effectiveness of educational administrators from inside and outside the teaching profession
   C. performance of administrators in the administration of public colleges
   D. degree of reality behind the nostalgia for scholarly pursuits often expressed by educational administrators

    2.____

3. According to the above passage, the value to an educational administrator of experience in the teaching profession
   A. lies in the first-hand knowledge he has acquired of immediate educational problems
   B. may lie in the belief of his colleagues, subordinates, and the public that such experience is necessary
   C. has been supported by evidence that the experience contributes to administrative success in educational fields
   D. would be greater if the administrator were able to free himself from nostalgia for his former duties

3._____

4. Of the following, the MOST suitable title for the above passage is
   A. Educational Administration, Its Problems
   B. The Experience Needed For Educational Administration
   C. Administration in Higher Education
   D. Evaluating Administrative Experience

4._____

Questions 5-6.

DIRECTIONS: Questions 5 and 6 are to be answered SOLELY on the basis of the following passage.

Management by objectives (MBO) may be defined as the process by which the superior and the subordinate managers of an organization jointly define its common goals, define each individual's major areas of responsibility in terms of the results expected of him and use these measure as guides for operating the unit and assessing the contribution of each of its members.

The MBO approach requires that after organizational goals are established and communicated, targets must be set for each individual position which are congruent with organizational goals. Periodic performance reviews and a final review using the objectives set as criteria are also basic to this approach.

Recent studies have shown that MBO programs are influenced by attitudes and perceptions of the boss, the company, the reward-punishment system, and the program itself. In addition, the manner in which the MBO program is carried out can influence the success of the program. A study done in the late sixties indicates that the best results are obtained when the manager sets goals which deal with significant problem areas in the organizational unit, or with the subordinate's personal deficiencies. These goals must be clear with regard to what is expected of the subordinate. The frequency of feedback is also important in the success of a management-by-objectives program. Generally, the greater the amount of feedback, the more successful the MBO program.

5. According to the above passage, the expected output for individual employees should be determined
   A. after a number of reviews of work performance
   B. after common organizational goals are defined
   C. before common organizational goals are defined
   D. on the basis of an employee's personal qualities

5._____

6. According to the above passage, the management-by-objectives approach requires
   A. less feedback than other types of management programs
   B. little review of on-the-job performance after the initial setting of goals
   C. general conformance between individual goals and organizational goals
   D. the setting of goals which deal with minor problem areas in the organization

Questions 7-10.

DIRECTIONS: Questions 7 through 10 are to be answered SOLELY on the basis of the following passage.

Management, which is the function of executive leadership, has as its principal phases the planning, organizing, and controlling of the activities of subordinate groups in the accomplishment of organizational objectives. Planning specifies the kind and extent of the factors, forces, and effects, and the relationships among them, that will be required for satisfactory accomplishment. The nature of the objectives and their requirements must be known before determinations can be made as to what must be done, how it must be done and why, where actions should take place, who should be responsible, and similar programs pertaining to the formulation of a plan. Organizing, which creates the conditions that must be present before the execution of the plan can be undertaken successfully, cannot be done intelligently without knowledge of the organizational objectives. Control, which has to do with the constraint and regulation of activities entering into the execution of the plan, must be exercised in accordance with the characteristics and requirements of the activities demanded by the plan.

7. The one of the following which is the MOST suitable title for the above passage is
   A. The Nature of Successful Organization
   B. The Planning of Management Functions
   C. The Importance of Organizational Functions
   D. The Principle Aspects of Management

8. It can be inferred from the above passage that the one of the following functions whose existence is essential to the existence of the other three is the
   A. regulation of the work needed to carry out a plan
   B. understanding of what the organization intends to accomplish
   C. securing of information of the factors necessary for accomplishment of objectives
   D. establishment of the conditions required for successful action

9. The one of the following which would NOT be included within any of the principal phases of the function of executive leadership as defined in the above passage is
   A. determination of manpower requirements
   B. procurement of required material
   C. establishment of organizational objectives
   D. scheduling of production

10. The conclusion which can MOST reasonably be drawn from the above passage is that the control phase of managing is most directly concerned with the
    A. influencing of policy determinations
    B. administering of suggestion systems
    C. acquisition of staff for the organization
    D. implementation of performance standards

Questions 11-12.

DIRECTIONS: Questions 11 and 12 are to be answered SOLELY on the basis of the following passage.

Under an open-and-above-board policy, it is to be expected that some supervisors will gloss over known shortcomings of subordinates rather than face the task of discussing team face-to-face. It is also to be expected that at least some employees whose job performance is below par will reject the supervisor's appraisal as biased and unfair. Be that as it may, these are inescapable aspects of any performance appraisal system in which human beings are involved. The supervisor who shies away from calling a spade a spade, as well as the employee with a chip on his shoulder, will each in his own way eventually be revealed in his true light—to the benefit of the organization as a whole.

11. The BEST of the following interpretations of the above passage is that
    A. the method of rating employee performance requires immediate revision to improve employee acceptance
    B. substandard performance ratings should be discussed with employees even if satisfactory ratings are not
    C. supervisors run the risk of being called unfair by the subordinates even though their appraisals are accurate
    D. any system of employee performance rating is satisfactory if used properly

12. The BEST of the following interpretations of the above passage is that
    A. supervisors generally are not open-and-above-board with their subordinates
    B. it is necessary for supervisors to tell employees objectively how they are performing
    C. employees complain when their supervisor does not keep them informed
    D. supervisors are afraid to tell subordinates their weaknesses

Questions 13-15.

DIRECTIONS: Questions 13 through 15 are to be answered SOLELY on the basis of the following passage.

During the last decade, a great deal of interest has been generated around the phenomenon of *organizational development,* or the process of developing human resources through conscious organization effort. Organizational development (OD) stresses improving interpersonal relationships and organizational skills, such as communication, to a much greater degree than individual training ever did. The kind of training that an organization should emphasize depends upon the present and future structure of the organization. If future organizations are to be unstable, shifting coalitions, then individual skills and abilities, particularly those emphasizing innovativeness, creativity, flexibility, and the latest technological knowledge, are crucial and individual training is most appropriate.

But if there is to be little change in organizational structure, then the main thrust of training should be group-oriented or organizational development. This approach seems better designed for overcoming hierarchical barriers, for developing a degree of interpersonal relationships which make communication along the chain of command possible, and for retaining a modicum of innovation and/or flexibility.

13. According to the above passage, group-oriented training is MOST useful in in
    A. developing a communications system that will facilitate understanding through the chain of command
    B. highly flexible and mobile organizations
    C. preventing the crossing of hierarchical barriers within an organization
    D. saving energy otherwise wasted on developing methods of dealing with rigid hierarchies

14. The one of the following conclusions which can be drawn MOST appropriately from the above passage is that
    A. behavioral research supports the use of organizational development training methods rather than individualized training
    B. it is easier to provide individualized training in specific skills than to set up sensitivity training programs
    C. organizational development eliminates innovative or flexible activity
    D. the nature of an organization greatly influences which training methods will be most effective

15. According to the above passage, the one of the following which is LEAST important for large-scale organizations geared to rapid and abrupt change is
    A. current technological information
    B. development of a high degree of interpersonal relationships
    C. development of individual skills and abilities
    D. emphasis on creativity

Questions 16-18.

DIRECTIONS: Questions 16 through 18 are to be answered SOLELY on the basis of the following passage.

The increase in the extent to which each individual is personally responsible to others is most noticeable in a large bureaucracy. No one person *decides* anything; each decision of any importance, is the product of an intricate process of brokerage involving individuals inside and outside the organization who feel some reason to be affected by the decision, or two have special knowledge to contribute to it. The more varied the organization's constituency, the more inside *veto-groups* will need to be taken into account. But even if no outside consultations were involved, sheer size would produce a complex process of decision. For a large organization is a deliberately created system of tensions into which each individual is expected to bring workways, viewpoints, and outside relationships markedly different from those of his colleagues. It is the administrator's task to draw from these disparate forces the elements of wise action from day to day, consistent with the purposes of the organization as a whole.

16. The above passage is essentially a description of decision-making as 16.____
    A. an organization process
    B. the key responsibility of the administrator
    C. the one best position among many
    D. a complex of individual decisions

17. Which one of the following statements BEST describes the responsibilities of an administrator? 17.____
    A. He modifies decisions and goals in accordance with pressures from within and outside the organization.
    B. He creates problem-solving mechanisms that rely on the varied interests of his staff and *veto-groups*.
    C. He makes determinations that will lead to attainment of his agency's objectives.
    D. He obtains agreement among varying viewpoints and interests

18. In the context of the operations of a central public personnel agency, a *veto-group* would LEAST likely consist of 18.____
    A. employee organizations
    B. professional personnel societies
    C. using agencies
    D. civil service newspapers

Questions 19-25.

DIRECTIONS: Questions 19 through 25 are to be answered SOLELY on the basis of the following passage, which is an extract from a report prepared for Department X, which outlines the procedure to be followed in the case of transfers of employees.

Every transfer, regardless of the reason therefore, requires completion of the record of transfer, Form DT411. To denote consent to the transfer, DT411 should contain the signatures of the transferee and the personnel officer(s) concerned, except that, in the case of an involuntary transfer, the signatures of the transferee's present and prospective supervisors shall be entered in Boxes 8A and 8B, respectively, since the transferee does not consent. Only a permanent employee may request a transfer; in such cases, the employee's attendance record shall be duly considered with regard to absences, latenesses, and accrued overtime balances. In the case of an inter-district transfer, the employee's attendance record must be included in Section 8A of the transfer request, Form DT410, by the personnel officer of the district from which the transfer is requested. The personnel officer of the district to which the employee requested transfer may refuse to accept accrued overtime balances in excess of ten days.

An employee on probation shall be eligible for transfer. If such employee is involuntarily transferred, he shall be credited for the period of time already served on probation. However, if such transfer is voluntary, the employee shall be required to serve the entire period of his probation in the new position. An employee who has occurred a disability which prevents him from performing his normal duties may be transferred during the period of such disability to other appropriate duties. A disability transfer requires the completion of either DT414 if the disability is job-connected, or Form DT415 if it is not a job-connected disability. In either case, the personnel officer of the district from which the transfer is made signs in Box 6A of the first two copies and the personnel officer of the district to which the transfer is made signs in Box 6B of the last two copies, or, in the case of an intra-district disability transfer, the personnel officer must sign in Box 6A of the first two copies and Box 6B of the last two copies.

19. When a personnel officer consents to an employee's request for transfer from his district, this procedure requires that the personnel officer sign Forms
    A. DT411
    B. DT410 and DT411
    C. DT411 and either Form DT414 or DT415
    D. DT410 and DT411, and either Form DT414 or DT415

20. With respect to the time record of an employee transferred against his wishes during his probationary period, this procedure requires that
    A. he serve the entire period of his probation in his present office
    B. he lose his accrued overtime balance
    C. his attendance record be considered with regard to absences and latenesses
    D. he be given credit for the period of time he has already served on probation

21. Assume you are a supervisor and an employee must be transferred into your office against his wishes.
    According to this procedure, the box you must sign on the record of transfer is
    A. 6A   B. 8A   C. 6B   D. 8B

22. Under this procedure, in the case of a disability transfer, when must Box 6A on Forms DT414 and DT415 be signed by the personnel officer of the district to which the transfer is being made?
    A. In all cases when either Form DT414 or Form DT415 is used
    B. In all cases when Form DT414 is used and only under certain circumstances when Form DT415 is used
    C. In all cases when Form DT415 is used and only under certain circumstances when Form DT414 is used
    D. Only under certain circumstances when either Form DT414 or Form DT415 is used

23. From the above passage, it may be inferred MOST correctly that the number of copies of Form DT414 is   23.____
    A. no more than 2
    B. at least 3
    C. at least 5
    D. more than the number of copies of Form DT415

24. A change in punctuation and capitalization only which would change one sentence into two and possibly contribute to somewhat greater ease of reading this report extract would be MOST appropriate in the   24.____
    A. 2nd sentence, 1st paragraph
    B. 3rd sentence, 1st paragraph
    C. next to the last sentence, 2nd paragraph
    D. 2nd sentence, 2nd paragraph

25. In the second paragraph, a word that is INCORRECTLY used is   25.____
    A. *shall* in the 1st sentence
    B. *voluntary* in the 3rd sentence
    C. *occurred* in the 4th sentence
    D. *intra-district* in the last sentence

KEY (CORRECT ANSWERS)

1.	C		11.	C
2.	B		12.	B
3.	B		13.	A
4.	B		14.	D
5.	B		15.	B
6.	C		16.	A
7.	D		17.	C
8.	B		18.	B
9.	C		19.	A
10.	D		20.	D

21. D
22. D
23. B
24. B
25. C

PREPARING WRITTEN MATERIAL

PARAGRAPH REARRANGEMENT
COMMENTARY

The sentences that follow are in scrambled order. You are to rearrange them in proper order and indicate the letter choice containing the correct answer at the space at the right.

Each group of sentences in this section is actually a paragraph presented in scrambled order. Each sentence in the group has a place in that paragraph; no sentence is to be left out. You are to read each group of sentences and decide upon the best order in which to put the sentences so as to form a well-organized paragraph.

The questions in this section measure the ability to solve a problem when all the facts relevant to its solution are not given.

More specifically, certain positions of responsibility and authority require the employee to discover connection between events sometimes, apparently, unrelated. In order to do this, the employee will find it necessary to correctly infer that unspecified events have probably occurred or are likely to occur. This ability becomes especially important when action must be taken on incomplete information.

Accordingly, these questions require competitors to choose among several suggested alternatives, each of which presents a different sequential arrangement of the events. Competitors must choose the MOST logical of the suggested sequences.

In order to do so, they may be required to draw on general knowledge to infer missing concepts or events that are essential to sequencing the given events. Competitors should be careful to infer only what is essential to the sequence. The plausibility of the wrong alternatives will always require the inclusion of unlikely events or of additional chains of events which are NOT essential to sequencing the given events.

It's very important to remember that you are looking for the best of the four possible choices, and that the best choice of all may not even be one of the answers you're given to choose from.

There is no one right way to solve these problems. Many people have found it helpful to first write out the order of the sentences, as they would have arranged them, on their scrap paper before looking at the possible answers. If their optimum answer is there, this can save them some time. If it isn't, this method can still give insight into solving the problem. Others find it most helpful to just go through each of the possible choices, contrasting each as they go along. You should use whatever method feels comfortable and works for you.

While most of these types of questions are not that difficult, we've added a higher percentage of the difficult type, just to give you more practice. Usually there are only one or two questions on this section that contain such subtle distinctions that you're unable to answer confidently. And you then may find yourself stuck deciding between two possible choices, neither of which you're sure about.

EXAMINATION SECTION
TEST 1

DIRECTIONS: The sentences that follow are in scrambled order. You are to rearrange them in proper order and indicate the letter choice containing the correct answer. *PRINT THE LETTER OF THE CORRECT ANSWER IN THE SPACE AT THE RIGHT.*

1. Below are four statements labeled W, X, Y and Z.
   W. He was a strict and fanatic drillmaster.
   X. The word is always used in a derogatory sense and generally shows resentment and anger on the part of the user.
   Y. It is from the name of this Frenchman that we derive our English word, martinet.
   Z. Jean Martinet was the Inspector-General of Infantry during the reign of King Louis XIV.
   The PROPER order in which these sentences should be placed in a paragraph is:
   A. X, Z, W, Y   B. X, Z, Y, W   C. Z, W, Y, X   D. Z, Y, W, X

   1.____

2. In the following paragraph, the sentences, which are numbered, have been jumbled.
   I. Since then it has undergone changes.
   II. It was incorporated in 1955 under the laws of the State of New York.
   III. Its primary purposes, a cleaner city, has, however, remained the same.
   IV. The Citizens Committee works in cooperation with the Mayor's Inter-departmental Committee for a Clean City.
   The order in which these sentences should be arranged to form a well-organized paragraph is:
   A. II, IV, I, III   B. III, IV, I, II   C. IV, II, I, III   D. IV, III, II, I

   2.____

   3.____

Questions 3-5.

DIRECTIONS: The sentences listed below are part of a meaningful paragraph but they are not given in their proper order. You are to decide what would be the BEST order in which to put the sentences so as to form a well-organized paragraph. Each sentence has a place in the paragraph; there are no extra sentences. You are then to answer Questions 3 through 5 inclusive on the basis of your rearrangements of these scrambled sentences into a properly organized paragraph.

In 1887 some insurance companies organized an Inspection Department to advise their clients on all phases of fire prevention and protection. Probably this has been due to the smaller annual fire losses in Great Britain than in the United States. It tests various fire prevention devices and appliances and determines manufacturing hazards and their safeguards. Fire research began earlier in the United States and is more advanced than in Great Britain. Later they established a laboratory specializing in electrical, mechanical, hydraulic, and chemical fields.

73

3. When the five sentences are arranged in proper order, the paragraph starts with the sentence which begins
    A. "In 1887…" B. "Probably this…" C. "It tests…"
    D. "Fire research…" E. "Later they…"

3.____

4. In the last sentence listed above, "they" refers to
    A. the insurance companies
    B. the United States and Great Britain
    C. the Inspection Department
    D. clients
    E. technicians

4.____

5. When the above paragraph is properly arranged, it ends with the words
    A. "…and protection."
    B. "…the United States."
    C. "…their safeguards."
    D. "…in Great Britain."
    E. "…chemical fields."

5.____

KEY (CORRECT ANSWERS)

1. C
2. C
3. D
4. A
5. C

TEST 2

DIRECTIONS: In each of the questions numbered I through V, several sentences are given. For each question, choose as your answer the group of number that represents the MOST logical order of these sentences if they were arranged in paragraph form. *PRINT THE LETTER OF THE CORRECT ANSWER IN THE SPACE AT THE RIGHT.*

1. I. It is established when one shows that the landlord has prevented the tenant's enjoyment of his interest in the property leased.
    II. Constructive eviction is the result of a breach of the covenant of quiet enjoyment implied in all leases.
    III. In some parts of the United States, it is not complete until the tenant vacates within a reasonable time.
    IV. Generally, the acts must be of such serious and permanent character as to deny the tenant the enjoyment of his possessing rights.
    V. In this event, upon abandonment of the premises, the tenant's liability for that ceases.
    The CORRECT answer is:
    A. II, I, IV, III, V
    B. V, II, III, I, IV
    C. IV, III, I, II, V
    D. I, III, V, IV, II

2. I. The powerlessness before private and public authorities that is the typical experience of the slum tenant is reminiscent of the situation of blue-collar workers all through the nineteenth century.
    II. Similarly, in recent years, this chapter of history has been reopened by anti-poverty groups which have attempted to organize slum tenants to enable them to bargain collectively with their landlords about the conditions of their tenancies.
    III. It is familiar history that many of the worker remedied their condition by joining together and presenting their demands collectively.
    IV. Like the workers, tenants are forced by the conditions of modern life into substantial dependence on these who possess great political aid and economic power.
    V. What's more, the very fact of dependence coupled with an absence of education and self confidence makes them hesitant and unable to stand up for what they need from those in power.
    The CORRECT answer is:
    A. V, IV, I, II, III
    B. II, III, I, V, IV
    C. III, I, V, IV, II
    D. I, IV, V, III, II

3. I. A railroad, for example, when not acting as a common carrier may contract away responsibility for its own negligence.
    II. As to a landlord, however, no decision has been found relating to the legal effect of a clause shifting the statutory duty of repair to the tenant.
    III. The courts have not passed on the validity of clauses relieving the landlord of this duty and liability.
    IV. They have, however, upheld the validity of exculpatory clauses in other types of contracts.

V. Housing regulations impose a duty upon the landlord to maintain leased premises in safe condition.
VI. As another example, a bailee may limit his liability except for gross negligence, willful acts, or fraud.

The CORRECT answer is:
A. II, I, VI, IV, III, V
B. I, III, IV, V, VI, II
C. III, V, I, IV, II, VI
D. V, III, IV, I, VI, II

4.
I. Since there are only samples in the building, retail or consumer sales are generally eschewed by mart occupants, and in some instances, rigid controls are maintained to limit entrance to the mart only to those persons engaged in retailing.
II. Since World War I, in many larger cities, there has developed a new type of property, called the mart building.
III. It can, therefore, be used by wholesalers and jobbers for the display of sample merchandise.
IV. This type of building is most frequently a multi-storied, finished interior property which is a cross between a retail arcade and a loft building.
V. This limitation enables the mart occupants to ship the orders from another location after the retailer or dealer makes his selection from the samples.

The CORRECT answer is:
A. II, IV, III, I, V
B. IV, III, V, I, II
C. I, III, II, IV, V
D. I, IV, II, III, V

5.
I. In general, staff-line friction reduces the distinctive contribution of staff personnel.
II. The conflicts, however, introduce an uncontrolled element into the managerial system.
III. On the other hand, the natural resistance of the line to staff innovations probably usefully restrains over-eager efforts to apply untested procedures on a large scale.
IV. Under such conditions, it is difficult to know when valuable ideas are being sacrificed.
V. The relatively weak position of staff, requiring accommodation to the line, tends to restrict their ability to engage in free, experimental innovation.

The CORRECT answer is:
A. IV, II, III, I, V
B. I, V, III, II, IV
C. V, III, I, II, IV
D. II, I, IV, V, III

KEY (CORRECT ANSWERS)

1. A
2. D
3. D
4. A
5. B

TEST 3

DIRECTIONS: Questions 1 through 4 consist of six sentences which can be arranged in a logical sequence. For each question, select the choice which places the numbered sentences in the MOST logical sequent. *PRINT THE LETTER OF THE CORRECT ANSWER IN THE SPACE AT THE RIGHT.*

1.
   I. The burden of proof as to each issue is determined before trial and remains upon the same party throughout the trial.
   II. The jury is at liberty to believe one witness' testimony as against a number of contradictory witnesses.
   III. In a civil case, the party bearing the burden of proof is required to prove his contention by a fair preponderance of the evidence.
   IV. However, it must be noted that a fair preponderance of evidence does not necessarily mean a greater number of witnesses.
   V. The burden of proof is the burden which rests upon one of the parties to an action to persuade the trier of the facts, generally the jury, that a proposition he asserts is true.
   VI. If the evidence is equally balanced, or if it leaves the jury in such doubt as to be unable to decide the controversy either way, judgment must be given against the party upon whom the burden of proof rests.

   The CORRECT answer is:
   A. III, II, V, IV, I, VI   B. I, II, VI, V, III, IV
   C. III, IV, V, I, II, VI   D. V, I, III, VI, IV, II

   1.____

2.
   I. If a parent is without assets and is unemployed, he cannot be convicted of the crime of non-support of a child.
   II. The term "sufficient ability" has been held to mean sufficient financial ability.
   III. It does not matter if his unemployment is by choice or unavoidable circumstances.
   IV. If he fails to take any steps at all, he may be liable to prosecution for endangering the welfare of a child.
   V. Under the penal law, a parent is responsible for the support of his minor child only if the parent is "of sufficient ability."
   VI. An indigent parent may meet his obligation by borrowing money or by seeking aid under the provisions of the Social Welfare Law

   The CORRECT answer is:
   A. VI, I, V, III, II, IV   B. I, III, V, II, IV, VI
   C. V, II, I, III, VI, IV   D. I, VI, IV, V, II, III

   2.____

3.
   I. Consider, for example, the case of a rabble rouser who urges a group of twenty people to go out and break the windows of a nearby factory.
   II. Therefore, the law fills the indicated gap with the crime of inciting to riot.
   III. A person is considered guilty of inciting to riot when he urges ten or more persons to engage in tumultuous and violent conduct of a kind likely to create public alarm.
   IV. However, if he has not obtained the cooperation of at least four people, he cannot be charged with unlawful assembly.

   3.____

77

V. The charge of inciting to riot was added to the law to cover types of conduct which cannot be classified as either the crime of "riot" or the crime of "unlawful assembly."
VI. If he acquires the acquiescence of at least four of them, he is guilty of unlawful assembly even if the project does not materialize.

The CORRECT answer is:
A. III, V, I, VI, IV, II
B. V, I, IV, VI, II, III
C. III, IV, I, V, II, VI
D. V, I, IV, VI, III, II

4.
I. If, however, the rebuttal evidence presents an issue of credibility, it is for the jury to determine whether the presumption has, in fact, been destroyed.
II. Once sufficient evidence to the contrary is introduced, the presumption disappears from the trial.
III. The effect of a presumption is to place the burden upon the adversary to come forward with evidence to rebut the presumption.
IV. When a presumption is overcome and ceases to exist in the case, the fact or facts which gave rise to the presumption still remain.
V. Whether a presumption has been overcome is ordinarily a question for the court.
VI. Such information may furnish a basis for a logical inference.

The CORRECT answer is:
A. IV, VI, II, V, I, III
B. III, II, V, I, IV, VI
C. V, III, VI, IV, II, I
D. V, IV, I, II, VI, III

4._____

KEY (CORRECT ANSWERS)

1. D
2. C
3. A
4. B

PREPARING WRITTEN MATERIAL
EXAMINATION SECTION
TEST 1

DIRECTIONS: The following groups of sentences need to be arranged in an order that makes sense. Select the letter preceding the sequence that represents the BEST sentence order. *PRINT THE LETTER OF THE CORRECT ANSWER IN THE SPACE AT THE RIGHT.*

1.
   I. A large Naval station on Alameda Island, near Oakland, held many warships in port, and the War Department was worried that if the bridge were to be blown up by the enemy, passage to and from the bay would be hopelessly blocked.
   II. Though many skeptics were opposed to the idea of building such an enormous bridge, the most vocal opposition came from a surprising source: the United States War Department.
   III. The War Department's concerns led to a showdown at San Francisco City Hall between Strauss and the Secretary of War, who demanded to know what would happen if a military enemy blew up the bridge.
   IV. In 1933, by submitting a construction cost estimate of $17 million, an engineer named Joseph Strauss won the contract to build the Golden Gate Bridge of San Francisco, which would then become one of the world's largest bridges.
   V. Strauss quickly ended the debate by explaining that the Golden Gate Bridge was to be a suspension bridge, whose roadway would hang in the air from cables strung between two huge towers, and would immediately sink into three hundred feet of water if it were destroyed.

   The BEST order is:
   A. II, III, I, IV, V   B. I, II, III, V, IV   C. IV, II, I, III, V   D. IV, I, III, V, II

   1.____

2.
   I. Plastic surgeons have already begun to use virtual reality to map out the complex nerve and tissue structures of a particular patient's face, in order to prepare for delicate surgery.
   II. A virtual reality program responds to these movements by adjusting the images that a person sees on a screen or through goggles, thereby creating an "interactive" world in which a person can see and touch three-dimensional graphic objects.
   III. No more than a computer program that is designed to build and display graphic images, the virtual reality program takes graphic programs a step further by sensing a person's head and body movements.
   IV. The computer technology known as virtual reality, now in its very first stages of development, is already revolutionizing some aspects of contemporary life.
   V. Virtual reality computers are also being used by the space program, most recently to simulate conditions for the astronauts who were launched on a repair mission to the Hubble telescope.

   2.____

The BEST order is:
A. IV, II, I, V, III   B. III, I, V, II, IV   C. IV, III, II, I, V   D. III, I, II, IV, V

3. I. Before you plant anything, the soil in your plant bed should be carefully raked level, a small section at a time, and any clods or rocks that can't be broken up should be removed.
    II. Your plant should be placed in a hole that will position it at the same level it was at the nursery, and a small indentation should be pressed into the soil around the plant in order to hold water near its roots.
    III. Before placing the plant in the soil, lightly separate any roots that may have been matted together in the container, cutting away any thick masses that can't be separated, so that the remaining roots will be able to grow outward.
    IV. After the bed is ready, remove your plant from its container by turning it upside down and tapping or pushing on the bottom —never remove it by pulling on the plant.
    V. When you bring home a small plant in an individual container from the nursery, there are several things to remember while preparing to plant it in your own garden.
    The BEST order is:
    A. V, IV, III, II, I   B. V, II, IV, III, II   C. I, IV, II, III, V   D. I, IV, V, II, III

4. I. The motte and its tower were usually built first, so that sentries could use it as a lookout to warn the castle workers of any danger that might approach the castle.
    II. Though the moat and palisade offered the bailey a good deal of protection, it was linked to the motte by a set of stairs that led to a retractable drawbridge at the motte's gate, to enable people to evacuate onto the motte in case of an attack.
    III. The motte of these early castles was a fortified hill, sometimes as high as one hundred feet, on which stood a palisade and tower.
    IV. The bailey was a clear, level spot below the motte, also enclosed by a palisade, which in turn was surrounded by a large trench or moat.
    V. The earliest castles built in Europe were not the magnificent stone giants that still tower over much of the European landscape, but simpler wooden constructions called motte-and-bailey castles.
    The BEST order is:
    A. V, III, I, IV, II   B. V, IV, I, II, III   C. I, IV, III, II, V   D. I, III, II, IV, V

5. I. If an infant is left alone or abandoned for a short while, its immediate response is to cry loudly, accompanying its screams with aggressive flailing of its legs and limbs.
    II. If a child has been abandoned for a longer period of time, it becomes completely still and quiet, as if realizing that now its only chance for survival is to shut its mouth and remain motionless.
    III. Along with their intense fear of the dark, the crying behavior of human infants offers insights into how prehistoric newborn children might have evolved instincts that would prevent them from becoming victims of predators.

IV. This behavior often surprises people who enter a hospital's maternity ward for the first time and encounter total silence from a roomful of infants.
V. This violent screaming response is quite different from an infant's cries of discomfort or hunger, and seems to serve as either the child's first line of defense against an unwanted intruder, or a desperate attempt to communicate its position to the mother.
The BEST order is:
A. III, II, IV, I, V B. III, I, V, II, IV C. I, V, IV, II, III D. II, IV, I, V, III

6. I. When two cats meet who are strangers, their first actions and gestures determine who the "dominant" cat will be, at least for the time being.
    II. Unlike dogs, cats are typically a solitary animal species who avoid social interaction, but they do display specific social responses to each other upon meeting.
    III. This is unlikely, however; before such a point of open hostility is reached, one of the cats will usually take the "submissive" position of crouching down while looking away from the other dat.
    IV. If a cat desires dominance or sees the other cat as a threat to its territory, it will stare directly at the intruder with a lowered tail.
    V. If the other cat responds with a similar gesture, or with the strong defensive posture of an arched back, laid-back ears and raised tail, a fight or chase is likely if neither cat gives in.
    The BEST order is:
    A. IV, II, I, V, III B. I, II, IV, V, III C. I, IV, V, III, II D. II, I, IV, V, III

7. I. A star or planet's gravitational force can best be explained in this way: anything passing through this "dent" in space will veer toward the star or planet as if it were rolling into a hole.
    II. Objects that are massive or heavy, such as stars or planets, "sink" into this surface, creating a sort of dent or concavity in the surrounding space.
    III. Black holes, the most massive objects known to exist in space, create dents so large and deep that the space surrounding them actually folds in on itself, preventing anything that falls in —even light —from ever escaping again.
    IV. The sort of dent a star or planet makes depends on how massive it is; planets generally have weak gravitational pulls, but stars, which are larger and heavier, make a bigger "dent" that will attract more matter.
    V. In outer space, the force of gravity works as if the surrounding space is a soft, flat surface.
    The BEST order is:
    A. III, V, II, I, IV B. III, IV, I, V, II C. V, II, I, IV, III D. I, V, II, IV, III

8. I. Eventually, the society of Kyoto gave the world one of its first and greatest novels when Japan's most promising writer, Lady Murasaki Shikibu, wrote her chronicle of Kyoto's society, *The Tale of Genji*, which preceded the first European novels by more than 500 years.
    II. The society of Kyoto was dedicated to the pleasures of art; the courtiers experimented with new and colorful methods of sculpture, painting, writing, decorative gardening, and even making clothes.

III. Japanese culture began under the powerful authority of Chinese Buddhism, which influenced every aspect of Japanese life from religion to politics and art.
IV. This new, vibrant culture was so sophisticated that all the people in Kyoto's imperial court considered themselves poets, and the line between life and art hardly existed —lovers corresponded entirely through written verses, and even government officials communicated by writing poems to each other.
V. In the eighth century, when the emperor established the town of Kyoto as the capital of the Japanese empire, Japanese society began to develop its own distinctive style.

The BEST order is:
A. V, II, IV, I, III   B. II, I, V, IV, III   C. V, III, IV, I, II   D. III, V, II, IV, I

9. I. Instead of wheels, the HSST uses two sets of magnets, one which sits on the track, and another that is carried by the train; these magnets generate an identical magnetic field which forces the two sets apart.
II. In the last few decades, railway travel has become less popular throughout the world, because it is much slower than travel by airplane, and not much less expensive.
III. The HSST's designers say that the train can take passengers from one town to another as quickly as a jet plane —while consuming less than half the energy.
IV. This repellent effect is strong enough to lift the entire train above the trackway, and the train, literally traveling on air, rockets along at speeds of up to 300 miles per hour.
V. The revolutionary technology of magnetic levitation, currently being tested by Japan's experimental HSST (High Speed Surface Transport), may yet bring passenger trains back from the dead.

The BEST order is:
A. II, V, I, IV, III   B. II, I, IV, III, V   C. V, II, III, I, IV   D. V, I, III, IV, II

10. I. When European countries first began to colonize the African continent, their impression of the African people was of a vast group of loosely organized tribal societies, without any great centralized source of power or wealth.
II. The legend of Timbuktu persisted until the nineteenth century, when a French adventurer visited Timbuktu and found that raids by neighboring tribesmen had made the city a shadow of its former self.
III. In the fifteenth century, when the stories of travelers who had traveled Africa's Sudan region began circulating around Europe, this impression began to change.
IV. In 1470, an Italian merchant named Benedetto Dei traveled to Timbuktu and confirmed these rumors, describing a thriving metropolis where rich and poor people worshipped together in the city's many ornate mosques — there was even a university in Timbuktu, much like its European counterparts, where African scholars pursued their studies in the arts and sciences.

V. The travelers' legends told of an enormous city in the western Sudan, Timbuktu, where the streets were crowded with goods brought by faraway caravans, and where there was a stone palace as large as any in Europe.

The BEST order is:
A. III, V, I, IV, II B. I, II, IV, III, V C. I, III, V, IV, II D. II, I, III, IV, V

11. I. Also, our reference points in sighting the moon make us believe that its size is changing; when the moon is rising through the trees, it seems huge, because our brains unconsciously compare the size of the moon with the size of the trees in the foreground.
    II. To most people, the sky itself appears more distant at the horizon than directly overhead, and if the moon's size—which remains constant—is projected from the horizon, the apparent distance of the horizon makes the moon look bigger.
    III. Up higher in the sky, the moon is set against tiny stars in the background, which will make the moon seem smaller.
    IV. People often wonder why the moon becomes bigger when it approaches the horizon, but most scientists agree that this is a complicated optical illusion, produced by at least three factors.
    V. The moon illusion may also be partially explained by a phenomenon that has nothing to do with errors in our perception—light that enters the earth's atmosphere is sometimes refracted, and so the atmosphere may act as a kind of magnifying glass for the moon's image.

    The BEST order is:
    A. IV, III, V, II, I B. IV, II, I, III, V C. V, II, I, III, IV D. II, I, III, IV, V

11.____

12. I. When the Native Americans were introduced to the horses used by white explorers, they were amazed at their new alternative—here was an animal that was strong and swift, would patiently carry a person or other loads on its back, and they later discovered, was right at home on the plains.
    II. Before the arrival of European explorers to North America, the natives of the American plains used large dogs to carry their travois-long lodgepoles loaded with clothing, gear, and food.
    III. These horses, it is now known, were not really strangers to North America; the very first horses originated here, on this continent, tens of thousands of years ago, and migrated into Asia across the Bering Land Bridge, a strip of land that used to link our continent with the Eastern world.
    IV. At first, the natives knew so little about horses that at least one tribe tried to feed their new animals pieces of dried meat and animal fat, and were surprised when the horses turned their heads away and began to eat the grass of the prairie.
    V. The American horse eventually became extinct, but its Asian cousins were reintroduced to the New World when the European explorers brought them to live among the Native Americans.

    The BEST order is:
    A. II, I, IV, III, V B. II, IV, I, III, V C. I, II, IV, III, V D. I, III, V, II, IV

12.____

13. I. The dress worn by the dancer is believed to have been adorned in the past by shells which would strike each other as the dancer performed, creating a lovely sound.
    II. Today's jingle-dress is decorated with the tin lids of snuff cans, which are rolled into cones and sewn onto the dress,
    III. During the jingle-dress dance, the dancer must blend complicated footwork with a series of gentle hos that cause the cones to jingle in rhythm to a drumbeat.
    IV. When contemporary Native American tribes meet for a pow-wow, one of the most popular ceremonies to take place is the women's jingle-dress dance.
    V. Besides being more readily available than shells, the lids are thought by many dancers to create a softer, more subtle sound.
    The BEST order is:
    A. II, IV, V, I, III   B. IV, II, I, III, V   C. II, I, III, V, IV   D. IV, I, II, V, III

14. I. If a homeowner lives where seasonal climates are extreme, deciduous shade trees—which will drop their leaves in the winter and allow sunlight to pass through the windows—should be planted near the southern exposure in order to keep the house cool during the summer.
    II. This trajectory is shorter and lower in the sky than at any other time of year during the winter, when a house most requires heating; the northern-facing parts of a house do not receive any direct sunlight at all.
    III. In designing an energy-efficient house, especially in colder climates, it is important to remember that most of the house's windows should face south.
    IV. Though the sun always rises in the east and sets in the west, the sun of the northern hemisphere is permanently situated in the southern portion of the sky.
    V. The explanation for why so many architects and builders want this "southern exposure" is related to the path of the sun in the sky.
    The BEST order is:
    A. III, I, V, IV, II   B. III, V, IV, II, I   C. I, III, IV, II, V   D. I, II, V, IV, III

15. I. His journeying lasted twenty-four years and took him over an estimated 75,000 miles, a distance that would not be surpassed by anyone other than Magellan—who sailed around the world—for another six hundred years.
    II. Perhaps the most far-flung of these lesser-known travelers was Ibn Batuta, an African Moslem who left his birthplace of Tangier in the summer of 1325.
    III. Ibn Batuta traveled all over Africa and Asia, from Niger to Peking, and to the islands of Maldive and Indonesia.
    IV. However, a few explorers of the Eastern world logged enough miles and adventures to make Marco Polo's voyage look like an evening stroll.
    V. In America, the most well-known of the Old World's explorers are usually Europeans such as Marco Polo, the Italian who brought many elements of Chinese culture to the Western world.
    The BEST order is:
    A. V, IV, II, III, I   B. V, IV, III, II, I   C. III, II, I, IV, V   D. II, III, I, IV, V

16.
   I. In the rainforests of South America, a rare species of frog practices a reproductive method that is entirely different from this standard process.
   II. She will eventually carry each of the tadpoles up into the canopy and drop each into its own little pool, where it will be easy to locate and safe from most predators.
   III. After fertilization, the female of the species, who lives almost entirely on the forest floor, lays between 2 and 16 eggs among the leaf litter at the base of a tree, and stands watch over these eggs until they hatch.
   IV. Most frogs are pond-dwellers who are able to deposit hundreds of eggs in the water and then leave them alone, knowing that enough eggs have been laid to insure the survival of some of their offspring.
   V. Once the tadpoles emerge, the female backs in among them, and a tadpole will wriggle onto her back to be carried high into the forest canopy, where the female will deposit it in a little pool of water cupped in the leaf of a plant.
   The BEST order is:
   A. I, IV, III, II, V   B. I, III, V, II, IV   C. IV, III, II, V, I   D. IV, I, III, V, II

16.____

17.
   I. Eratosthenes had heard from travelers that at exactly noon on June 21, in the ancient city of Aswan, Egypt, the sun cast no shadow in a well, which meant that the sun must be directly overhead.
   II. He knew the sun always cast a shadow in Alexandria, and so he figured that if he could measure the length of an Alexandria shadow at the time when there was no shadow in Aswan, he could calculate the angle of the sun, and therefore the circumference of the earth.
   III. The evidence for a round earth was not new in 1492; in fact, Eratosthenes, an Alexandrian geographer who lived nearly sixteen centuries before Columbus's voyage (275-195 B.C.), actually developed a method for calculating the circumference of the earth that is still in use today.
   IV. Eratosthenes's method was correct, but his result—28,700 miles—was about 15 percent too high, probably because of the inaccurate ancient methods of keeping time, and because Aswan was not due south of Alexandria, as Eratosthenes had believed.
   V. When Christopher Columbus sailed across the Atlantic Ocean for the first time in 1492, there were still some people in the world who ignored scientific evidence and believed that the earth was flat, rather than round.
   The BEST order is:
   A. I, II, V, III, IV   B. V, III, IV, I, II   C. V, III, I, II, IV   D. III, V, I, II, IV

17.____

18.
   I The first name for the child is considered a trial naming, often impersonal and neutral, such as the Ngoni name *Chabwera*, meaning "it has arrived."
   II. This sort of name is not due to any parental indifference to the child, but is a kind of silent recognition of Africa's sometimes high infant death rate; most parents ease the pain of losing a child with the belief that it is not really a person until it has been given a final name.
   III. In many tribal African societies, families often give two different names to their children, at different periods in time.
   IV. After the trial naming period has subsided and it is clear that the child will survive, the parents choose a final name for the child, an act that symbolically completes the act of birth.

18.____

V. In fact, some African first-given names are explicitly uncomplimentary, translating as "I am dead" or "I am ugly," in order to avoid the jealousy of ancestral spirits who might wish to take a child that is especially healthy or attractive.

The BEST order is:
A. III, I, II, V, IV
B. III, IV, II, I, V
C. IV, III, I, II, V
D. IV, V, III, I, II

19.
I. Though uncertain of the definite reasons for this behavior, scientists believe the birds digest the clay in order to counteract toxins contained in the seeds of certain fruits that are eaten by macaws.
II. For example, all macaws flock to riverbanks at certain times of the year to eat the clay that is found in river mud.
III. The macaws of South America are not only among the largest and most beautifully colored of the world's flying birds, but they are also one of the smartest.
IV. It is believed that macaws are forced to resort to these toxic fruits during the dry season, when foods are more scarce.
V. The macaw's intelligence has led to intense study by scientists, who have discovered some macaw behaviors that have not yet been explained.

The BEST order is:
A. III, IV, I, II, V
B. III, V, II, I, IV
C. V, II, I, IV, III
D. IV, I, II, III, V

20.
I. Although Maggie Kuhn has since passed away, the Gray Panthers are still waging a campaign to reinstate the historical view of the elderly as people whose experience allows them to make their greatest contribution in their later years.
II. In 1972, an elderly woman named Maggie Kuhn responded to this sort of treatment by forming a group called the Gray Panthers, an organization of both old and young adults with the common goal of creating change.
III. This attitude is reflected strongly in the way elderly people are treated by our society; many are forced into early retirement, or are placed in rest homes in which they are isolated from their communities.
IV. Unlike most other cultures around the world, Americans tend to look upon old age with a sense of dread and sadness.
V. Kuhn believed that when the elderly are forced to withdraw into lives that lack purpose, society loses one of its greatest resources: people who have a lifetime of experience and wisdom to offer their communities.

The BEST order is:
A. IV, III, II, V, I
B. IV, II, I, III, V
C. II, IV, III, V, I
D. II, I, IV, III, V

21.
I. The current theory among most anthropologists is that humans evolved from apes who lived in trees near the grasslands of Africa.
II. Still, some anthropologists insist that such an invention was necessary for the survival of early humans, and point to the Kung Bushmen of central Africa as a society in which the sling is still used in this way.
III. Two of these inventions—fire, and weapons such as spears and clubs—were obvious defenses against predators, and there is archaeological evidence to support the theory of their use.

IV. Once people had evolved enough to leave the safety of trees and walk upright, they needed the protection of several inventions in order to survive.
V. But another invention, a feather or fiber sling that allowed mothers to carry children while leaving their hands free to gather roots or berries, would certainly have decomposed and left behind no trace of itself.

The BEST order is:
A. I, II, III, V, IV B. IV, I, II, III, V C. I, IV, III, V, II D. IV, III, V, II, I

22. I. The person holding the bird should keep it in hot water up to its neck, and the person cleaning should work a mild solution of dishwashing liquid into the bird's plumage, paying close attention to the head and neck.
II. When rinsing the bird, after all the oil has been removed, the running water should be directed against the lay of its feathers, until water begins to bead off the surface of the feathers—a sign that all the detergent has been rinsed out.
III. If you have rescued a sea bird from an oil spill and want to restore it to clean and normal living, you need a large sink, a constant supply of running hot water (a little over 100°F), and regular dishwashing liquid.
IV. This cleaning with detergent solution should be repeated as many times as it takes to remove all traces of oil from the bird's feathers, sometime over a period of several days.
V. But before you begin to clean the bird, you must find a partner because cleaning an oiled bird is a two-person job.

The BEST order is:
A. III, I, II, IV, V B. III, V, I, IV, II C. III, I, IV, V, II D. III, IV, V, I, II

23. I. The most difficult time of year for the Tsaatang is the spring calving, when the reindeer leave their wintering ground and rush to their accustomed calving place, without stopping by night or by day.
II. Reindeer travel in herds, and though some animals are tamed by the Tsaatang for riding or milking, the herds are allowed to roam free.
III. This journey is hard for the Tsaatang, who carry all their possessions with them, but once it's over it proves worthwhile; the Tsaatang can immediately begin to gather milk from reindeer cows who have given birth.
IV. The Tsaatang, a small tribe who live in the far northwest corner of Mongolia, practice a lifestyle that is completely dependent on the reindeer, their main resource for food, clothing, and transport.
V. The people must follow their yearly migrations, living in portable shelters that resemble Native American tepees.

The BEST order is:
A. I, III, II, V, IV B. I, IV, II, V, III C. IV, I, III, V, II D. IV, II, V, I, III

24. I. The Romans later improved this system by installing these heated pipe networks throughout walls and ceilings, supplying heat to even the uppermost floors of a building—a system that, to this day, hasn't been much improved.
II. Air-conditioning, the method by which humans control indoor temperatures, was practiced much earlier than most people think.

III. The earliest heating devices other than open fires were used in 350 B.C. by the ancient Greeks, who directed air that had been heated by underground fires into baked clay pipes that ran under the floor.
IV. Ironically, the first successful cooling system, patented in England in 1831, used fire as its main energy source—fires were lit in the attic of a building, creating an updraft of air that drew cool air into the building through ducts that had underground openings near the river Thames.
V. Cooling buildings was more of a challenge, and wasn't attempted until 1500: a water-based system, designed by Leonardo da Vinci, does not appear to have been successful, since it was never used again.

The BEST order is:
A. III, V, IV, I, II   B. III, I, II, V, IV   C. II, III, I, V, IV   D. IV, II, III, I, V

25. I. Cold, dry air from Canada passes over the Rocky Mountains and sweeps down onto the plains, where it collides with warm, moist air from the waters of the Gulf of Mexico, and when the two air masses meet, the resulting disturbance sometimes forms a violent funnel cloud that strikes the earth and destroys virtually everything in its path.
II. Hurricanes, storms which are generally not this violent and last much longer, are usually given names by meteorologists, but this tradition cannot be applied to tornados, which have a life span measured in minutes and disappear in the same way as they are born—unnamed.
III. A tornado funnel forms rotating columns of air whose speed reaches three hundred miles an hour—a speed that can only be estimated, because no wind-measuring devices in the direct path of a storm have ever survived.
IV. The natural phenomena known as tornados occur primarily over the Midwestern grasslands of the United States.
V. It is here, meteorologists tell us, that conditions for the formation of tornados are sometimes perfect during the spring months.

The BEST order is:
A. II IV, V, I, III   B. II, III, I, V, IV   C. IV, V, I, III, II   D. IV, III, I, V, II

11 (#1)

KEY (CORRECT ANSWERS)

1.	C	11.	B
2.	C	12.	A
3.	B	13.	D
4.	A	14.	B
5.	B	15.	A
6.	D	16.	D
7.	C	17.	C
8.	D	18.	A
9.	A	19.	B
10.	C	20.	A

21. C
22. B
23. D
24. C
25. C

PREPARING WRITTEN MATERIAL
EXAMINATION SECTION
TEST 1

DIRECTIONS: Each of Questions 1 through 5 consists of a sentence which may or may not be an example of good formal English usage. Examine each sentence, considering grammar, punctuation, spelling, capitalization, and awkwardness. Then choose the correct statement about it from the four options below it. If the English usage in the sentence given is better than any of the changes suggested in options B, C, or D, pick option A. (Do not pick an option that will change the meaning of the sentence.) *PRINT THE LETTER OF THE CORRECT ANSWER IN THE SPACE AT THE RIGHT.*

1. I don't know who could possibly of broken it.   1.____
    A. This is an example of good formal English usage.
    B. The word "who" should be replaced by the word "whom."
    C. The word "of" should be replaced by the word "have."
    D. The word "broken" should be replaced by the word "broke."

2. Telephoning is easier than to write.   2.____
    A. This is an example of good formal English usage.
    B. The word "telephoning" should be spelled "telephoneing."
    C. The word "than" should be replaced by the word "then."
    D. The words "to write" should be replaced by the word "writing."

3. The two operators who have been assigned to these consoles are on vacation.   3.____
    A. This is an example of good formal English usage.
    B. A comma should be placed after the word "operators."
    C. The word "who" should be replaced by the word "whom."
    D. The word "are" should be replaced by the word "is."

4. You were suppose to teach me how to operate a plugboard.   4.____
    A. This is an example of good formal English usage.
    B. The word "were" should be replaced by the word "was."
    C. The word "suppose" should be replaced by the word "supposed."
    D. The word "teach" should be replaced by the word "learn."

5. If you had taken my advice; you would have spoken with him.   5.____
    A. This is an example of good formal English usage.
    B. The word "advice" should be spelled "advise."
    C. The words "had taken" should be replaced by the word "take."
    D. The semicolon should be changed to a comma.

KEY (CORRECT ANSWERS)

1. C
2. D
3. A
4. C
5. D

TEST 2

DIRECTIONS: Select the correct answer. *PRINT THE LETTER OF THE CORRECT ANSWER IN THE SPACE AT THE RIGHT.*

1. The one of the following sentences which is MOST acceptable from the viewpoint of correct grammatical usage is:
   A. I do not know which action will have worser results.
   B. He should of known better.
   C. Both the officer on the scene, and his immediate supervisor, is charged with the responsibility.
   D. An officer must have initiative because his supervisor will not always be available to answer questions.

   1.____

2. The one of the following sentences which is MOST acceptable from the viewpoint of correct grammatical usage is:
   A. Of all the officers available, the better one for the job will be picked.
   B. Strict orders were given to all the officers, except he.
   C. Study of the law will enable you to perform your duties more efficiently.
   D. It seems to me that you was wrong in failing to search the two men.

   2.____

3. The one of the following sentences which does NOT contain a misspelled word is:
   A. The duties you will perform are similar to the duties of a patrolman.
   B. Officers must be constantly alert to sieze the initiative.
   C. Officers in this organization are not entitled to special privileges.
   D. Any changes in procedure will be announced publically.

   3.____

4. The one of the following sentences which does NOT contain a misspelled word is:
   A. It will be to your advantage to keep your firearm in good working condition.
   B. There are approximately fourty men on sick leave.
   C. Your first duty will be to pursuade the person to obey the law.
   D. Fires often begin in flameable material kept in lockers.

   4.____

5. The one of the following sentences which does NOT contain a misspelled word is:
   A. Offices are not required to perform technical maintainance.
   B. He violated the regulations on two occasions.
   C. Every employee will be held responable for errors.
   D. This was his nineth absence in a year.

   5.____

KEY (CORRECT ANSWERS)

1. D
2. C
3. C
4. A
5. B

TEST 3

DIRECTIONS: Select the correct answer. *PRINT THE LETTER OF THE CORRECT ANSWER IN THE SPACE AT THE RIGHT.*

1. You are answering a letter that was written on the letterhead of the ABC Company and signed by James H. Wood, Treasurer.
   What is usually considered to be the correct salutation to use in your reply?
   A. Dear ABC Company:
   B. Dear Sirs:
   C. Dear Mr. Wood:
   D. Dear Mr. Treasurer:

   1.____

2. Assume that one of your duties is to handle routine letters of inquiry from the public.
   The one of the following which is usually considered to be MOST desirable in replying to such a letter is a
   A. detailed answer handwritten on the original letter of inquiry
   B. phone call, since you can cover details more easily over the phone than in a letter
   C. short letter giving the specific information requested
   D. long letter discussing all possible aspects of the question raised

   2.____

3. The CHIEF reason for dividing a letter into paragraphs is to
   A. make the message clear to the reader by starting a new paragraph for each new topic
   B. make a short letter occupy as much of the page as possible
   C. keep the reader's attention by providing a pause from time to time
   D. make the letter look neat and businesslike

   3.____

4. Your superior has asked you to send an e-mail from your agency to a government agency in another city. He has written out the message and has indicated the name of the government agency.
   When you dictate the message to your secretary, which of the following items that your superior has NOT mentioned must you be sure to include?
   A. Today's date
   B. The full address of the government agency
   C. A polite opening such as "Dear Sirs"
   D. A final sentence such as "We would appreciate hearing from your agency in reply as soon as is convenient for you"

   4.____

5. The one of the following sentences which is grammatically preferable to the others is:
   A. Our engineers will go over your blueprints so that you may have no problems in construction.
   B. For a long time he had been arguing that we, not he, are to blame for the confusion.
   C. I worked on this automobile for two hours and still cannot find out what is wrong with it.
   D. Accustomed to all kinds of hardships, fatigue seldom bothers veteran policemen.

   5.____

KEY (CORRECT ANSWERS)

1. C
2. C
3. A
4. B
5. A

TEST 4

DIRECTIONS: Select the correct answer. *PRINT THE LETTER OF THE CORRECT ANSWER IN THE SPACE AT THE RIGHT.*

1. Suppose that an applicant for a job as snow laborer presents a letter from a former employer stating: "John Smith has a pleasing manner and never got into an argument with his fellow employees. He was never late or absent."
   This letter
   A. indicates that with some training Smith will make a good snow gang boss
   B. presents no definite evidence of Smith's ability to do snow work
   C. proves definitely that Smith has never done any snow work before
   D. proves definitely that Smith will do better than average work as a snow laborer

   1.____

2. Suppose you must write a letter to a local organization in your section refusing a request in connection with collection of their refuse.
   You should start the letter by
   A. explaining in detail the consideration you gave the request
   B. praising the organization for its service to the community
   C. quoting the regulation which forbids granting the request
   D. stating your regret that the request cannot be granted

   2.____

3. Suppose a citizen writes in for information as to whether or not he may sweep refuse into the gutter. A Sanitation officer answers as follows:
   Dear Sir:
   No person is permitted to litter, sweep, throw or cast, or direct, suffer or permit any person under his control to litter, sweep, throw or cast any ashes, garbage, paper, dust, or other rubbish or refuse into any public street or place, vacant lot, air shaft, areaway, backyard or court.
   Very truly yours,
   John Doe
   This letter is *poorly* written CHIEFLY because
   A. the opening is not indented   B. the thought is not clear
   C. the tone is too formal and cold   D. there are too many commas used

   3.____

4. A section of a disciplinary report written by a Sanitation officer states: "It is requested that subject Sanitation man be advised that his future activities be directed towards reducing his recurrent tardiness else disciplinary action will be initiated which may result in summary discharge."
   This section of the report is *poorly* written MAINLY because
   A. at least one word is misspelled   B. it is not simply expressed
   C. more than one idea is expressed   D. the purpose is not stated

   4.____

5. A section of a disciplinary report written by an officer states: "He comes in late. He takes too much time for lunch. He is lazy. I recommend his services be dispensed with."
   This section of the report is *poorly* written MAINLY because
   A. it ends with a preposition   B. it is not well organized
   C. no supporting facts are stated   D. the sentences are too simple

   5.____

KEY (CORRECT ANSWERS)

1. B
2. D
3. C
4. B
5. C

EDUCATING AND INTERACTING WITH THE PUBLIC

These questions test for knowledge of techniques used to interact effectively with individual citizens and/or community groups, to educate or inform them about topics of concern, to publicize or clarify agency programs or policies, to negotiate conflicts or resolve complaints, and to represent one's agency or program in a manner in keeping with good public relations practices. Questions may also cover interacting with others in cooperative efforts of public outreach or service. There will be 15 questions in this subject area on the written test.

TEST TASK:
You will be presented with a variety of situations in which you must apply knowledge of how best to interact with other people.

SAMPLE QUESTION:
A person approaches you expressing anger about a recent action by your department. Which one of the following should be your first response to this person?

    A. Interrupt to say you cannot discuss the situation until he calms down.
    B. Say you are sorry that he has been negatively affected by your department's action.
    C. Listen and express understanding that he has been upset by your department's action.
    D. Give him an explanation of the reasons for your department's action.

The correct answer to this sample question is choice C

C. SOLUTION:

Choice A *is not correct.* It would be inappropriate to interrupt. In addition, saying that you cannot discuss the situation until the person calms down will likely aggravate him further.

Choice B *is not correct.* Apologizing for your department's action implies that the action was improper.

Choice C is the correct answer to this question. By listening and expressing understanding that your department's action has upset him, you demonstrate that you have heard and understand his feelings and point of view.

Choice D *is not correct.* While an explanation of the reasons for the action may be appropriate at a later time, at this moment the person is angry and would not be receptive to such an explanation.

SAMPLE QUESTIONS

COMMUNICATING WITH THE PUBLIC

DIRECTIONS: Each question or incomplete statement is followed by several suggested answers or completions. Select the one that BEST answers the question or completes the statement. *PRINT THE LETTER OF THE CORRECT ANSWER IN THE SPACE AT THE RIGHT.*

1. If others are within hearing distance while you are taking a confidential phone message, the BEST way to verify that the message is correct is to
   A. read the message back to the caller
   B. ask the caller to call back later
   C. explain that you will call back
   D. ask the caller to repeat the message

   1.____

2. In order to complete a certain task, you need to ask a favor of a worker you don't know very well. The BEST way to do this would be to
   A. ask him briefly stating your reasons
   B. convince him it is for the good of the office
   C. tell him how greatly he can benefit if he does it
   D. offer to do something for him in return

   2.____

KEY (CORRECT ANSWERS)

1. The correct answer is D. If the caller repeats the message to you, the other people in the room will not hear what he is saying, and you will be able to check the facts in the message.

2. The correct answer is A. Be businesslike and to the point when you ask for a work-related favor from a fellow worker.

EXAMINATION SECTION

TEST 1

DIRECTIONS: Each question or incomplete statement is followed by several suggested answers or completions. Select the one that BEST answers the question or completes the statement. *PRINT THE LETTER OF THE CORRECT ANSWER IN THE SPACE AT THE RIGHT.*

1. Which of the following is a behavior that can impact customer service? 1._____
   A. Greeting customers promptly
   B. Believing in a positive mission statement
   C. Giving great service
   D. Poor work attitude

2. What are vital behaviors? 2._____
   A. Ones that are mandated by law
   B. Specific actions that have the maximum impact on customer service
   C. Of no particular importance when influencing employees
   D. The same as good attitudes

3. Of the following, the MOST effective icebreaker when greeting a local citizen in your office would be: 3._____
   A. Talking about local interests such as a sports team or the weather
   B. Expression appreciation for the citizen visiting you today
   C. Finding out and expressing interest in something the citizen shows interest in
   D. All of the above

4. Which of the following actions would get citizens to interact with you and, therefore, the government you represent? 4._____
   A. Inviting the citizens to fill out a survey on government services
   B. Helping the citizen find answers to questions about your department
   C. Both A and B
   D. None of the above

5. Of the following options, the BIGGEST issue with not greeting a citizen promptly is: 5._____
   A. He or she might not leave as quickly as you'd like them to
   B. The department misses an opportunity to establish a positive relationship
   C. They may estimate that their wait was shorter than it actually was
   D. Both A and C

6. Which of the following actions is important to take when someone makes an oral presentation to a large group of local residents? 6._____
   A. Relax the audience by moving back and forth when speaking
   B. Avoid eye contact with anyone in the audience
   C. Speak loudly enough for all to hear your message
   D. Turn your back to the audience when presenting visual aids

7. Of the following techniques for writing effective communication (i.e., letters about local tax bills) to residents, which of the following helps a person consistently stay on message the MOST?
   A. Preparing outlines
   B. Development and inclusion of charts
   C. Consulting references
   D. Asking questions

8. Persuasive messages that ask a person to do something should be communicated in a way that makes it easy for that person to
   A. plan accordingly
   B. answer politely
   C. organize logically
   D. respond positively

9. If a city department wishes to emphasize customer service skills such as courtesy and friendliness, when should said department focus on these skills?
   A. When designing their facilities
   B. During market research
   C. When meeting for technology planning
   D. During the hiring process

10. If a department realizes it needs to improve its technology to better meet resident demands and desires, this would have to result from a business activity known as
    A. continuity improvement
    B. business process management
    C. employee training and in-service
    D. organizational positioning

11. When in the distribution channel business, what is an important thing to keep in mind concerning customers?
    A. Most expect low service levels
    B. Many want immediate delivery
    C. Everyone defines service differently
    D. A number of customers tend to refuse late shipments

12. When persuading a citizen to go along with a proposed change from their initial query, you should
    A. explain how the change will benefit them
    B. tell them you have a better way of doing things
    C. minimize the amount of information you share with them
    D. reinforce your ideas with facts and statistics

13. Which of the following statements is TRUE regarding use of the internet to administer questionnaires?
    A. Interviewers are more likely to influence respondents' answers online
    B. Online questionnaires require more time for data entry and collection
    C. Respondents are more likely to misunderstand online questionnaires
    D. Data entry and administrative costs are higher for online questionnaires

14. After a series of notable scandals, a government organization wants the public to perceive it as more trustworthy and embarks on an advertising campaign to aid the makeover. What goal does this illustrate?
    A. Projecting a certain image
    B. Achieving stability
    C. Increasing customer service and productivity
    D. All of the above

14.____

15. When presenting information to a small group of town residents, you decide to use presentation software to prepare your multimedia presentation. What is the purpose of using this software?
    A. To develop websites
    B. To maintain customer files
    C. To access online resources
    D. To support your report findings

15.____

16. A current trend in interaction with citizens in order to build loyal customer relationships and enhance service levels focuses on optimizing the use of
    A. independent agents
    B. internet web sites
    C. satellite roving devices
    D. service rating advisors

16.____

17. Which of the following would be an excellent example of a parks department official empathizing with a citizen's objection?
    A. "I understand how you feel."
    B. "You must think the price is too high."
    C. "Everyone knows this is how this process works."
    D. "I really don't see what you don't understand about this."

17.____

18. Customer service experts who use the services and products they are in charge of dispensing are able to suggest appropriate substitute services and products because of their own personal
    A. preference
    B. feelings
    C. experience
    D. opinion

18.____

19. An official should always attempt to answer a citizen's questions thoroughly and explain the benefits of their services so that the citizen will
    A. make a quicker decision
    B. be in a state of indecision
    C. think about making a decision
    D. feel better about the decision

19.____

20. One should be able to adjust his customer-service style from one citizen to another so that he can appeal to each citizen's
    A. natural aptitude
    B. unique personality
    C. hidden objection
    D. internal ability

20.____

21. In order to attract local residents and encourage them to make use of a new recreation facility, what should a parks department director do?
    A. Market the site's benefits
    B. Host trade shows
    C. Distribute press kits
    D. Host special community events

21.____

22. What kind of question is a person asking if they ask the following: "What level of service would you like today?"   22.____
   A. Interpretive
   B. Impersonal
   C. Open-ended
   D. Assumptive

23. Your department holds a meeting to identify community issues with which they can involve themselves.   23.____
   Which of the following options should the department consider when deciding which community issue to involve themselves with?
   It should
   A. contribute to the social good
   B. earn a reasonable profit
   C. boost loyalty among citizens
   D. support controversial topics

24. If a person's thoughts, emotions and physical sensations interfere with their listening skills, that is referred to as   24.____
   A. cultural diversity
   B. internal noise
   C. cultural norms
   D. external noise

25. Which of the following is NOT a characteristic of information literacy?   25.____
   The ability to
   A. use information to manipulate others
   B. determine what information is needed for a presentation
   C. find information relevant to a topic
   D. use information to create new knowledge

KEY (CORRECT ANSWERS)

1.	A	11.	C
2.	B	12.	A
3.	D	13.	C
4.	C	14.	A
5.	B	15.	D
6.	C	16.	B
7.	A	17.	A
8.	D	18.	C
9.	D	19.	D
10.	B	20.	B

21. D
22. C
23. A
24. B
25. A

TEST 2

DIRECTIONS: Each question or incomplete statement is followed by several suggested answers or completions. Select the one that BEST answers the question or completes the statement. *PRINT THE LETTER OF THE CORRECT ANSWER IN THE SPACE AT THE RIGHT.*

1. When preparing to deliver a speech, what is the purpose of writing key points on notecards and then placing those cards in order of their importance?
   A. To verify their authenticity
   B. To access files
   C. To revise facts
   D. To organize information

   1.____

2. A city official who is originally from Ecuador meets with a citizen who has moved to the area from London, England. When the official attempts to shake the citizen's hand, he backs away.
   What cultural issue should the official be aware of next time to avoid this misstep?
   A. Punctuality
   B. Personal space preferences
   C. Appearance
   D. Language variances

   2.____

3. Someone who demonstrates self-confidence has which of the following characteristics?
   A. They take few risks because they fear making mistakes
   B. They exhibit aggressive behavior when expressing their opinion
   C. They realize that mistakes are a part of personal growth
   D. They are overly concerned with what others say about them

   3.____

4. A town clerk is talking with a resident about fees associated with filing a building permit when the resident interrupts and says, "I refuse to pay for this. These fees are preposterous!"
   If the clerk wishes to reply in the most professional manner possible, they should do which of the following?
   A. Attempt to explain the benefits of the service
   B. Stop helping the resident and find someone else to help
   C. Ask a supervisor to help convince the resident of the service's merits
   D. Thank the resident politely for coming in

   4.____

5. You are working with a village resident who asks you questions about aspects of zoning ordinances that you are clearly not familiar with. A coworker overhears the conversation and offers to help.
   What is the FIRST thing you should do?
   A. Politely refuse the help and attempt to answer the resident's questions anyway
   B. Accept the offer of help and listen to the answers the coworker gives to the resident
   C. Ignore the coworker; they only want to look good in front of your supervisor
   D. Let the other associate take over and look for a new resident to help

   5.____

6. A resident comes up to an employee in the public works department holding his village-issued recycling container. He says he received the pail a month ago and it already has a cracked handle. As a result his lawn is constantly littered with plastic bottles.
   What is the FIRST thing the employee should say?
   A. "There's no reason it should be cracked. We should have another; I will check for you."
   B. "We've never had anyone make this complaint before. What did you or your child do to it?"
   C. "Are you sure you the village provided this pail? Do you have a receipt?"
   D. "We've had a lot of issues with that item. You should probably contact the manufacturer."

6._____

7. When a person first encounters an employee and forms a lasting mental image of that employee and, therefore, the organization, that is called
   A. attitude impact   B. self-confidence
   C. first impression   D. workplace ethics

7._____

8. Which of the following convey to citizens that their representative is professional?
   A. No wrinkles, creases or stains   B. No large, loud prints
   C. Well-tailored, formal clothing   D. All of the above

8._____

9. A town clerk is put in charge of email communications for the department and asks you for help.
   Which of the following would NOT be considered good email etiquette?
   A. Keeping emails brief and to the point
   B. Putting the purpose of the email in the subject field
   C. Sending humorous YouTube videos and personal emails to customers
   D. Using a signature that includes contact information that follows your message

9._____

10. A building department director is holding a meeting for individual building managers and is just about to conclude when another manager shows up late.
    Which of the following actions would be the BEST to take?
    A. Thank the manager for stopping by and pause the meeting momentarily to fill him or her in on what they missed.
    B. Once the meeting is over, remind the manager that punctuality is incredibly important to your department. Then once they seem to understand the importance of being on time, fill them in on what they missed.
    C. Openly criticize the manager in front of everyone else for being tardy. Once you've criticized them, fill them in on what they missed.
    D. Slightly nod to the manager when they enter, but continue the meeting without bringing them up to speed. Once the meeting concludes, fill the manager in if the wish to be brought up to speed.

10._____

11. You are running 15 minutes late to a meeting with a constituent.
    What should you do?
    A. Call the constituent and tell them you will be there in a few minutes.
    B. The constituent won't mind waiting. Fifteen minutes is not that long of a wait.
    C. Have your coworker talk to the constituent and tell them you were involved in a minor traffic accident that is causing you to be delayed.
    D. Pretend like you thought the meeting was supposed to be on a different day. Send an email apologizing for the inconvenience.

    11._____

12. A longtime friend has stopped at your work to visit you before they fly home. You are currently meeting with the local civic association when he shows up.
    What should you do?
    A. Have your friend join the meeting and introduce him to the group.
    B. Tell your friend to wait in the break room/cafeteria and meet him when you finish up your meeting.
    C. Stop the meeting immediately and tell the group to reschedule with you tomorrow. You also let them know they will have priority in terms of meeting times.
    D. Speed through the rest of the meeting and do not stop to ask if anyone has any questions. Then find your friend afterwards.

    12._____

13. A fellow clerk is filling out forms with a local resident when you notice your favorite song starts playing from your computer. You
    A. dance around the office after blasting the music on your speakers
    B. listen to the music with your headphones at a loud volume so that the clerk and resident can hear a muted version of the song
    C. listen to the music with your headphones in at a low volume so that you do not disturb others and are still accessible in case you are needed
    D. listen to your music with noise-cancelling headphones, so that you cannot hear others if they request your attention

    13._____

14. As recreation director, you have an important meeting with members of a local youth sports organization and all agree to meet around dinner time.
    Where should you bring them for the dinner meeting?
    A. Ask them their preference for food and pick the corresponding restaurant
    B. An upscale French restaurant known for its romantic ambience
    C. A sports bar that will be airing an important playoff game
    D. Order Chinese food and invite them to the office

    14._____

15. A city employee has an important presentation in front of a community group today, but it is also "Casual Friday."
    How should the employee dress? Why?
    A. Dress casually. The residents will understand that Casual Fridays are for casual dress, so they will not be upset.
    B. Business casual. A city employee wants to assure the community that they handle business the way they dress, which means a smart, but comfortable look.

    15._____

C. A little nicer than normally, but nothing too formal. This way they are still comfortable, but the residents know that they are important too.
D. Dress in pajamas. The group does not care what an employee wears as long as their presentation is good.

16. Professionally, what is the longest it should take someone to respond to a resident's email? How about a phone call?
   A. 45 minutes; 15 minutes
   B. 24 hours; 24 hours
   C. 48 hours; 24 hours
   D. 24 hours; 4 hours

16._____

17. Unlike social etiquette, office and business professionalism are PRIMARILY based on
   A. hierarchy and power
   B. personal relations between employees and customers
   C. common sense and courtesy
   D. both A and C

17._____

18. If something goes wrong during interaction with or presentation for a local community group, what should you do?
   A. Clear your head, focus, and be cheerful and professional and act like nothing went wrong
   B. Take responsibility and take appropriate action
   C. Blame others for your technical difficulties
   D. Find a way to end the interaction as quickly as possible

18._____

19. What is the ultimate goal of customer service?
   A. Customer satisfaction
   B. Understanding customers
   C. Identify problems
   D. Improve product and service

19._____

20. Of the following, which is the BEST reason for office employees and supervisors to frequently gauge customer satisfaction?
   A. No reason. One evaluation is enough.
   B. Because employees are not always honest about reporting customer satisfaction.
   C. They may have concerns or complaints that they have not voiced.
   D. Complaints do not always reach management.

20._____

21. Which of the following is TRUE of scope of influence?
   A. It is objective.
   B. Some have a larger scope of influence than others.
   C. Everyone has the same scope of influence.
   D. It is not relevant to customer service.

21._____

22. Which of the following techniques will create credibility in the minds of local residents in regards to their government representatives?
   A. Never admit being wrong. It undermines credibility.
   B. Demonstrate your human emotions. Whether you're angry or happy, let others see it.

22._____

C. Tell people what they want to hear even if it is not necessarily what you know to be true.
D. Become an expert about various factors in your profession. People will respect your knowledge.

23. You are in a "train the trainer" meeting about meeting customer expectations. As you talk in small groups after a short presentation, four people express very different statements about customer expectations.
Which one is CORRECT?
    A. "Wrong. Customer expectations are always changing."
    B. "Customer expectations rarely change."
    C. "Guys, all you really have to do is make a promise to solve customer problems. They forget after a while, even if you don't follow through."
    D. "Do not worry about what other companies are doing. We should focus on ourselves."

23.____

24. Of the following, which of the following is TRUE concerning customer service?
    A. Average customer service will always suffice.
    B. Customers lost through poor customer service are easy to replace.
    C. Organizations must provide excellent customer service or expect failure.
    D. None of the above

24.____

25. You are in a tense conversation with a very upset and aggressive resident. How should you handle this situation?
    A. Make them respect and value your time.
    B. Avoid admitting any wrongdoing on your part.
    C. Find a solution and implement it.
    D. Do not show empathy.

25.____

KEY (CORRECT ANSWERS)

1.	D		11.	A
2.	B		12.	B
3.	C		13.	C
4.	A		14.	A
5.	B		15.	B
6.	A		16.	D
7.	C		17.	D
8.	D		18.	B
9.	C		19.	A
10.	D		20.	C

21. B
22. D
23. A
24. C
25. C

EXAMINATION SECTION
TEST 1

DIRECTIONS: Each question or incomplete statement is followed by several suggested answers or completions. Select the one that BEST answers the question or completes the statement. *PRINT THE LETTER OF THE CORRECT ANSWER IN THE SPACE AT THE RIGHT.*

1. In public agencies, communications should be based PRIMARILY on a
    A. two-way flow from the top down and from the bottom up, most of which should be given in writing to avoid ambiguity
    B. multi-direction flow among all levels and with outside persons
    C. rapid, internal one-way flow from the top down
    D. two-way flow of information, most of which should be given orally for purposes of clarity

1._____

2. In some organizations, changes in policy or procedures are often communicated by word of mouth from supervisors to employees with no prior discussion or exchange of viewpoints with employees.
   This procedure often produces employee dissatisfaction CHIEFLY because
    A. information is mostly unusable since a considerable amount of time is required to transmit information
    B. lower-level supervisors tend to be excessively concerned with minor details
    C. management has failed to seek employees' advice before making changes
    D. valuable staff time is lost between decision-making and the implementation of decisions

2._____

3. For good letter writing, you should try to visualize the person to whom you are writing, especially if you know him.
   Of the following rules, it is LEAST helpful in such visualization to think of
    A. the person's likes and dislikes, his concerns, and his needs
    B. what you would be likely to say if speaking in person
    C. what you would expect to be asked if speaking in person
    D. your official position in order to be certain that your words are proper

3._____

4. One approach to good informal letter writing is to make letters and conversational.
   All of the following practices will usually help to do this EXCEPT:
    A. If possible, use a style which is similar to the style used when speaking
    B. Substitute phrases for single words (e.g., *at the present time* for *now*)
    C. Use contractions of words (e.g., *you're* for *you are*)
    D. Use ordinary vocabulary when possible

4._____

5. All of the following rules will aid in producing clarity in report-writing EXCEPT:
   A. Give specific details or examples, if possible
   B. Keep related words close together in each sentence
   C. Present information in sequential order
   D. Put several thoughts or ideas in each paragraph

6. The one of the following statements about public relations which is MOST accurate is that
   A. in the long run, appearance gains better results than performance
   B. objectivity is decreased if outside public relations consultants are employed
   C. public relations is the responsibility of every employee
   D. public relations should be based on a formal publicity program

7. The form of communication which is usually considered to be MOST personally directed to the intended recipient is the
   A. brochure   B. film   C. letter   D. radio

8. In general, a document that presents an organization's views or opinions on a particular topic is MOST accurately known as a
   A. tear sheet   B. position paper
   C. flyer   D. journal

9. Assume that you have been asked to speak before an organization of persons who oppose a newly announced program in which you are involved. You feel tense about talking to this group.
   Which of the following rules generally would be MOST useful in gaining rapport when speaking before the audience?
   A. Impress them with your experience
   B. Stress all areas of disagreement
   C. Talk to the group as to one person
   D. Use formal grammar and language

10. An organization must have an effective public relations program since, at its best, public relations is a bridge to change.
    All of the following statements about communication and human behavior have validity EXCEPT:
    A. People are more likely to talk about controversial matters with like-minded people than with those holding other views
    B. The earlier an experience, the more powerful its effect since it influences how later experiences will be interpreted
    C. In periods of social tension, official sources gain increased believability
    D. Those who are already interested in a topic are the ones who are most open to receive new communications about it

11. An employee should be encouraged to talk easily and frankly when he is dealing with his supervisor.
    In order to encourage such free communication, it would be MOST appropriate for a supervisor to behave in a(n)
    A. sincere manner; assure the employee that you will deal with him honestly and openly
    B. official manner; you are a supervisor and must always act formally with subordinates
    C. investigative manner; you must probe and question to get to a basis of trust
    D. unemotional manner; the employee's emotions and background should play no part in your dealings with him

12. Research findings show that an increase in free communication within an agency GENERALLY results in which one of the following?
    A. Improved morale and productivity
    B. Increased promotional opportunities
    C. An increase in authority
    D. A spirit of honesty

13. Assume that you are a supervisor and your superiors have given you a new-type procedure to be followed.
    Before passing this information on to your subordinates, the one of the following actions that you should take FIRST is to
    A. ask your superiors to send out a memorandum to the entire staff
    B. clarify the procedure in your own mind
    C. set up a training course to provide instruction on the new procedure
    D. write a memorandum to your subordinates

14. Communication is necessary for an organization to be effective.
    The one of the following which is LEAST important for most communication systems is that
    A. messages are sent quickly and directly to the person who needs them to operate
    B. information should be conveyed understandably and accurately
    C. the method used to transmit information should be kept secret so that security can be maintained
    D. senders of messages must know how their messages are received and acted upon

15. Which one of the following is the CHIEF advantage of listening willingly to subordinates and encouraging them to talk freely and honestly?
    It
    A. reveals to supervisors the degree to which ideas that are passed down are accepted by subordinates
    B. reduces the participation of subordinates in the operation of the department
    C. encourages subordinates to try for promotion
    D. enables supervisors to learn more readily what the *grapevine* is saying

16. A supervisor may be informed through either oral or written reports. 16.____
    Which one of the following is an ADVANTAGE of using oral reports?
    A. There is no need for a formal record of the report.
    B. An exact duplicate of the report is not easily transmitted to others.
    C. A good oral report requires little time for preparation.
    D. An oral report involves two-way communication between a subordinate and his supervisor.

17. Of the following, the MOST important reason why supervisors should 17.____
    communicate effectively with the public is to
    A. improve the public's understanding of information that is important for them to know
    B. establish a friendly relationship
    C. obtain information about the kinds of people who come to the agency
    D. convince the public that services are adequate

18. Supervisors should generally NOT use phrases like *too hard*, *too easy*, and 18.____
    a lot PRINCIPALLY because such phrases
    A. may be offensive to some minority groups
    B. are too informal
    C. mean different things to different people
    D. are difficult to remember

19. The ability to communicate clearly and concisely is an important element in 19.____
    effective leadership.
    Which of the following statements about oral and written communication is
    GENERALLY true?
    A. Oral communication is more time-consuming.
    B. Written communication is more likely to be misinterpreted.
    C. Oral communication is useful only in emergencies.
    D. Written communication is useful mainly when giving information to fewer than twenty people.

20. Rumors can often have harmful and disruptive effects on an organization. 20.____
    Which one of the following is the BEST way to prevent rumors from becoming a
    problem?
    A. Refuse to act on rumors, thereby making them less believable.
    B. Increase the amount of information passed along by the *grapevine*.
    C. Distribute as much factual information as possible.
    D. Provide training in report writing.

21. Suppose that a subordinate asks you about a rumor he has heard. The rumor 21.____
    deals with a subject which your superiors consider *confidential*.
    Which of the following BEST describes how you should answer the
    subordinate? Tell

A. the subordinate that you don't make the rules and that he should speak to higher ranking officials
B. the subordinate that you will ask your superior for information
C. him only that you cannot comment on the matter
D. him the rumor is not true

22. Supervisors often find it difficult to *get their message across* when instructing newly appointed employees in their various duties.
The MAIN reason for this is generally that the
    A. duties of the employees have increased
    B. supervisor is often so expert in his area that he fails to see it from the learner's point of view
    C. supervisor adapts his instruction to the slowest learner in the group
    D. new employees are younger, less concerned with job security and more interested in fringe benefits

23. Assume that you are discussing a job problem with an employee under your supervision. During the discussion, you see that the man's eyes are turning away from you and that he is not paying attention.
In order to get the man's attention, you should FIRST
    A. ask him to look you in the eye
    B. talk to him about sports
    C. tell him he is being very rude
    D. change your tone of voice

24. As a supervisor, you may find it necessary to conduct meetings with your subordinates.
Of the following, which would be MOST helpful in assuring that a meeting accomplishes the purpose for which it was called?
    A. Give notice of the conclusions you would like to reach at the start of the meeting.
    B. Delay the start of the meeting until everyone is present.
    C. Write down points to be discussed in proper sequence.
    D. Make sure everyone is clear on whatever conclusions have been reached and on what must be done after the meeting.

25. Every supervisor will occasionally be called upon to deliver a reprimand to a subordinate. If done properly, this can greatly help an employee improve his performance.
Which one of the following is NOT a good practice to follow when giving a reprimand?
    A. Maintain your composure and temper
    B. Reprimand a subordinate in the presence of other employees so they can learn the same lesson
    C. Try to understand why the employee was not able to perform satisfactorily
    D. Let your knowledge of the man involved determine the exact nature of the reprimand

KEY (CORRECT ANSWERS)

1.	C	11.	A
2.	B	12.	A
3.	D	13.	B
4.	B	14.	C
5.	D	15.	A
6.	C	16.	D
7.	C	17.	A
8.	B	18.	C
9.	C	19.	B
10.	C	20.	C

21. B
22. B
23. D
24. D
25. B

TEST 2

DIRECTIONS: Each question or incomplete statement is followed by several suggested answers or completions. Select the one that BEST answers the question or completes the statement. *PRINT THE LETTER OF THE CORRECT ANSWER IN THE SPACE AT THE RIGHT.*

1. Usually one thinks of communication as a single step, essentially that of transmitting an idea.
   Actually, however, this is only part of a total process, the FIRST step of which should be
   A. the prompt dissemination of the idea to those who may be affected by it
   B. motivating those affected to take the required action
   C. clarifying the idea in one's own mind
   D. deciding to whom the idea is to be communicated

   1.____

2. Research studies on patterns of informal communication have concluded that most individuals in a group tend to be passive recipients of news, while a few make it their business to spread it around in an organization.
   With this conclusion in mind, it would be MOST correct for the supervisor to attempt to identify these few individuals and
   A. give them the complete facts on important matters in advance of others
   B. inform the other subordinates of the identity of these few individuals so that their influence may be minimized
   C. keep them straight on the facts on important matters
   D. warn them to cease passing along any information to others

   2.____

3. The one of the following which is the PRINCIPAL advantage of making an oral report is that it
   A. affords an immediate opportunity for two-way communication between the subordinate and superior
   B. is an easy method for the superior to use in transmitting information to others of equal rank
   C. saves the time of all concerned
   D. permits more precise pinpointing of praise or blame by means of follow-up questions by the superior

   3.____

4. An agency may sometimes undertake a public relations program of a defensive nature.
   With reference to the use of defensive public relations, it would be MOST correct to state that it
   A. is bound to be ineffective since defensive statements, even though supported by factual data, can never hope to even partly overcome the effects of prior unfavorable attacks
   B. proves that the agency has failed to establish good relationships with newspapers, radio stations, or other means of publicity

   4.____

2 (#2)

      C. shows that the upper echelons of the agency have failed to develop sound public relations procedures and techniques
      D. is sometimes required to aid morale by protecting the agency from unjustified criticism and misunderstanding of policies or procedures

5. Of the following factors which contribute to possible undesirable public attitudes towards an agency, the one which is MOST susceptible to being changed by the efforts of the individual employee in an organization is that
      A. enforcement of unpopular regulations as offended many individuals
      B. the organization itself has an unsatisfactory reputation
      C. the public is not interested in agency matters
      D. there are many errors in judgment committed by individual subordinates

5.____

6. It is not enough for an agency's services to be of a high quality; attention must also be given to the acceptability of these services to the general public.
This statement is GENERALLY
      A. *false*; a superior quality of service automatically wins public support
      B. *true*; the agency cannot generally progress beyond the understanding and support of the public
      C. *false*; the acceptance by the public of agency services determines their quality
      D. *true*; the agency is generally unable to engage in any effective enforcement activity without public support

6.____

7. Sustained agency participation in a program sponsored by a community organization is MOST justified when
      A. the achievement of agency objectives in some area depends partly on the activity of this organization
      B. the community organization is attempting to widen the base of participation in all community affairs
      C. the agency is uncertain as to what the community wants
      D. the agency is uncertain as to what the community wants

7.____

8. Of the following, the LEAST likely way in which a records system may serve a supervisor is in
      A. developing a sympathetic and cooperative public attitude toward the agency
      B. improving the quality of supervision by permitting a check on the accomplishment of subordinates
      C. permit a precise prediction of the exact incidences in specific categories for the following year
      D. helping to take the guesswork out of the distribution of the agency

8.____

9. Assuming that the *grapevine* in any organization is virtually indestructible, the one of the following which it is MOST important for management to understand is:
    A. What is being spread by means of the *grapevine* and the reason for spreading it
    B. What is being spread by means of the *grapevine* and how it is being spread
    C. Who is involved in spreading the information that is on the *grapevine*
    D. Why those who are involved in spreading the information are doing so

9.____

10. When the supervisor writes a report concerning an investigation to which he has been assigned, it should be LEAST intended to provide
    A. a permanent official record of relevant information gathered
    B. a summary of case findings limited to facts which tend to indicate the guilt of a suspect
    C. a statement of the facts on which higher authorities may base a corrective or disciplinary action
    D. other investigators with information so that they may continue with other phases of the investigation

10.____

11. In survey work, questionnaires rather than interviews are sometimes used. The one of the following which is a DISADVANTAGE of the questionnaire method as compared with the interview is the
    A. difficulty of accurately interpreting the results
    B. problem of maintaining anonymity of the participant
    C. fact that it is relatively uneconomical
    D. requirement of special training for the distribution of questionnaires

11.____

12. in his contacts with the public, an employee should attempt to create a good climate of support for his agency.
    This statement is GENERALLY
    A. *false*; such attempts are clearly beyond the scope of his responsibility
    B. *true*; employees of an agency who come in contact with the public have the opportunity to affect public relations
    C. *false*; such activity should be restricted to supervisors trained in public relations techniques
    D. *true*; the future expansion of the agency depends to a great extent on continued public support of the agency

12.____

13. The repeated use by a supervisor of a call for volunteers to get a job done is objectionable MAINLY because it
    A. may create a feeling of animosity between the volunteers and the non-volunteers
    B. may indicate that the supervisor is avoiding responsibility for making assignments which will be most productive
    C. is an indication that the supervisor is not familiar with the individual capabilities of his men
    D. is unfair to men who, for valid reasons, do not, or cannot volunteer

13.____

14. Of the following statements concerning subordinates' expressions to a supervisor of their opinions and feelings concerning work situations, the one which is MOST correct is that
    A. by listening and responding to such expressions the supervisor encourages the development of complaints
    B. the lack of such expressions should indicate to the supervisor that there is a high level of job satisfaction
    C. the more the supervisor listens to and responds to such expressions, the more he demonstrates lack of supervisory ability
    D. by listening and responding to such expressions, the supervisor will enable many subordinates to understand and solve their own problems on the job

15. In attempting to motivate employees, rewards are considered preferable to punishment PRIMARILY because
    A. punishment seldom has any effect on human behavior
    B. punishment usually results in decreased production
    C. supervisors find it difficult to punish
    D. rewards are more likely to result in willing cooperation

16. In an attempt to combat the low morale in his organization, a high level supervisor publicized an *open-door policy* to allow employees who wished to do so to come to him with their complaints.
    Which of the following is LEAST likely to account for the fact that no employee came in with a complaint?
    A. Employees are generally reluctant to go over the heads of their immediate supervisor.
    B. The employees did not feel that management would help them.
    C. The low morale was not due to complaints associated with the job.
    D. The employees felt that they had more to lose than to gain.

17. It is MOST desirable to use written instructions rather than oral instructions for a particular job when
    A. a mistake on the job will not be serious
    B. the job can be completed in a short time
    C. there is no need to explain the job minutely
    D. the job involves many details

18. If you receive a telephone call regarding a matter which your office does not handle, you should FIRST
    A. give the caller the telephone number of the proper office so that he can dial again
    B. offer to transfer the caller to the proper office
    C. suggest that the caller re-dial since he probably dialed incorrectly
    D. tell the caller he has reached the wrong office and then hang up

19. When you answer the telephone, the MOST important reason for identifying yourself and your organization is to
    A. give the caller time to collect his or her thoughts
    B. impress the caller with your courtesy
    C. inform the caller that he or she has reached the right number
    D. set a business-like tone at the beginning of the conversation

19.____

20. As soon as you pick up the phone, a very angry caller begins immediately to complain about city agencies and *red tape*. He says that he has been shifted to two or three different offices. It turs out that he is seeking information which is not immediately available to you. You believe, you know, however, where it can be found.
    Which of the following actions is the BEST one for you to take?
    A. To eliminate all confusion, suggest that the caller write the agency stating explicitly what he wants.
    B. Apologize by telling the caller how busy city agencies now are, but also tell him directly that you do not have the information he needs.
    C. Ask for the caller's telephone number and assure him you will call back after you have checked further.
    D. Give the caller the name and telephone number of the person who might be able to help, but explain that you are not positive he will get results/

20.____

21. Which of the following approaches usually provides the BEST communication in the objectives and values of a new program which is to be introduced?
    A. A general written description of the program by the program manager for review by those who share responsibility
    B. An effective verbal presentation by the program manager to those affected
    C. Development of the plan and operational approach in carrying out the program by the program manager assisted by his key subordinates
    D. Development of the plan by the program manager's supervisor

21.____

22. What is the BEST approach for introducing change?
    A
    A. combination of written and also verbal communication to all personnel affected by the change
    B. general bulletin to all personnel
    C. meeting pointing out all the values of the new approach
    D. written directive to key personnel

22.____

23. Of the following, committees are BEST used for
    A. advising the head of the organization
    B. improving functional work
    C. making executive decisions
    D. making specific planning decisions

23.____

24. An effective discussion leader is one who
    A. announces the problem and his preconceived solution at the start of the discussion
    B. guides and directs the discussion according to pre-arranged outline
    C. interrupts or corrects confused participants to save time
    D. permits anyone to say anything at any time

25. The human relations movement in management theory is basically concerned with
    A. counteracting employee unrest
    B. eliminating the *time and motion* man
    C. interrelationships among individuals in organizations
    D. the psychology of the worker

KEY (CORRECT ANSWERS)

1.	C	11.	A
2.	C	12.	B
3.	A	13.	B
4.	D	14.	D
5.	D	15.	D
6.	B	16.	C
7.	A	17.	D
8.	C	18.	B
9.	A	19.	C
10.	B	20.	C

21.	C
22.	A
23.	A
24.	B
25.	C

BASIC FUNDAMENTALS OF INTERPERSONAL RELATIONSHIPS

TABLE OF CONTENTS

	Page
INSTRUCTIONAL OBJECTIVES	1
CONTENT	1
INTRODUCTION	1
1. Interpersonal Conduct and Behavior on the Job	1
Formal Organization of the Office	2
Office as a Setting for Formal and Informal Relations	2
Office Behavior	2
2. Interpersonal Communication – The Meaning	3
Importance of Face-to-Face Contacts	3
Listening Techniques	3
3. Factors in Interpersonal Communication	3
The Choice of Words of the Conversant	4
How Each Sees Each Other	4
The Right Time and Place	4
The Effect of Past Experience	4
The Effect of Personal Differences	5
4. Defense Mechanisms in Interpersonal Relations	5
Causes for Defense Mechanisms	5
Results of Use of Defense Mechanisms	5
5. Influences of Role Playing in Interpersonal Relations	6
Exploring Superior-Subordinate Relations	6
Interpersonal Relations Achieved Through Simulation	7
6. Measuring Interpersonal Relations	7
Survey of Interpersonal Values	7
Analysis of Interpersonal Behavior	8
STUDENT LEARNING ACTIVITIES	8
TEACHER MANAGEMENT ACTIVITIES	9
EVALUATION QUESTIONS	10

BASIC FUNDAMENTALS OF INTERPERSONAL RELATIONSHIPS

INSTRUCTIONAL OBJECTIVES

1. Ability to distinguish between formal and informal behavior.
2. Ability to identify the important factors in communicating with people.
3. Ability to understand how defense mechanisms affect communication with others.
4. Ability to identify the roles played in effective person-to-person communication.
5. Ability to acquire the human relations skills needed for getting along with others both on and off the job.
6. Ability to establish greater personal effectiveness with others so as to develop better cooperation and superior-subordinate relationships in public-service working situations.
7. Ability to recognize the mutual dependence of individuals on each other.
8. Ability to form positive attitudes toward the worth and dignity of every human being.
9. Ability to become aware of how feelings affect one's own behavior, as well as one's relationships with other people.
10. Ability to use an understanding of human relationships to effectively work with people.
11. Ability to improve communications with others by developing greater effectiveness in dealing with people in the world of public service.

CONTENT

INTRODUCTION

Perhaps the single most important skill that a public-service worker, or anyone for that matter, needs, is the ability to get along with other people. "Person-to-person" relationships are the building blocks of all social interactions between two-individuals. If there is one essential ingredient for success in life, both on and off the job, it is developing greater effectiveness in dealing with people.

The skill of the teacher is critical to the success of this unit. He should establish a permissive and non-threatening group climate in which free communication and behavior can take place. The importance of this unit cannot be over stated. The overall objective is to establish greater personal effectiveness with others and to develop better co-operative and superior-subordinate relationships in the public-service occupations. Obtaining greater "self-awareness" is a large part of this goal. Because interpersonal relations are affected by a variety of factors, some attention should be given initially to basic rules of conduct and behavior on the job.

1. INTERPERSONAL CONDUCT AND BEHAVIOR ON THE JOB

Most public-service agencies have clearly defined rules and regulations. The behavior of the public-service worker is often guided by the established procedures and directives of that individual agency. In many cases, even individual departments or units will have procedures manuals, which regulate conduct and office work.

Formal Organization of the Office

At one point or another, most public-service employees either work directly in an office, or come in frequent contact with other people working in an administrative or staff office. Students should become familiar with the organizational structure of the occupational groups in which they are planning on working. A park worker, for example, must know about the organization of the Parks Department—what kinds of staff or administrative services are provided, what about training, what are the safety rules, what goes into personnel records, etc. Preparing a flow chart of the relationships between different positions in a particular agency is one way of learning about the organization of that office or agency.

Office as a Setting for formal and Informal Relations

It is necessary to become aware of the different kinds of social relations shared with co-workers and the public. Some co-workers, for example, are seen only at work, and others are seen socially after work and/or on weekends. Factors that determine which co-workers become *personal* friends and which are just *work* friends should be considered and discussed.

On the other hand, a public-service worker usually has more formal relationships with the public with whom he comes into contact. Consider the relationships of the preschool teacher's aide and his students, the library helper and his library patrons, the police cadet and the general public, etc. In each of these cases, the public expects the public-service worker to help them with a particular service.

Although the distinction between formal and informal social relationships is not always clear, one should be sensitive to the fact that both kinds of relationships affect the behavior of the public and the public-service employee, Normally, the very organization of the public-service office helps to create a social climate for developing working relationships of a formal nature, and personal relationships with co-workers and the public which are of a more impersonal nature.

Office Behavior

Specific kinds of behavior relate to these formal and informal relationships with other people. Typically, the formal relationship is well prescribed and regulated by procedures or directives. The license interviewer, as an example, has specific questions to ask, and specific information to obtain from the applicant. Their relationship can be described as formal or prescribed by regulation. On the other hand, other office behavior can best be described as informal and non-prescribed (or *free*). Interpersonal relations in this case are often more personal and relaxed by their very nature.

2. INTERPERSONAL COMMUNICATION - THE MEANING

   Interpersonal communication can be defined as a two-way flow of information from person-to-person. One cannot Study human relations without examining the constant relationships that man has with other people; the individual does not exist in a vacuum. Most of man's psychological and social needs are met through dealings with other people. In fact, one psychiatrist (Harry Stark Sullivan) has developed a theory of personality based upon interpersonal situations. This viewpoint, known as the *Interpersonal Theory of Psychiatry,* claims that personality is essentially the enduring pattern of continued interpersonal relationships between people. This interpersonal behavior is all that can be observed as personality.

   Importance of Face-to-Face Contacts

   The very phrase. *Public Service Occupations,* suggests frequent face-to-face contacts with not only the general public, but with co-workers as well. With possibly a few exceptions, practically every public-service employee encounters frequent person-to-person contacts both on and off the job. The ability to get along with people is a very important part of public-service work.

   Listening Techniques

   Effective listening is a critical part of interpersonal communications. Listening is an active process, requiring not only that one must *pay attention* to what is being said, but that one must also *listen* for the meaning of what is being said. Almost one-half of the total time spent communicating, (reading, writing, speaking, or listening) is spent in listening.

   Even though people get considerable practice at listening, they don't do too well at it. Many studies have shown that, on the average, a person retains only about 25 percent of a given speech after only 10 minutes have elapsed. Most people forget three quarters of what they hear in a relatively short period of time. Clearly, people need to improve their listening skills if they are to become more effective in their relations with other people.

3. FACTORS IN INTERPERSONAL COMMUNICATION
   There are a number of components that affect the person-to-person relationship. Some of the factors common to both the sender and the receiver in a person-to-person communication are:

   The Attitudes and Emotions of the Individuals

   For example - two people are shouting and screaming at each other - how effective is their interpersonal communication?

   - *The Needs and Wants of the People Communicating*

Both the sender and receiver have unique desires, some open, and some hidden from the other person. These needs can and do strongly influence interpersonal relationships.

- *The Implied Demands of the Sender and Receiver*

An important factor in interpersonal communications involves requests or demands. How are these demands handled? What are some typical responses to demands? These factors are common to both the sender and the receiver in interpersonal relations and affect the individual behavior of the people communicating.

The Choice of Words of the Conversant

One's choice of words can have a direct bearing on the interpersonal communication. The vocabulary one uses in interpersonal relationships should be appropriate for the occasion. For example, a preschool teacher's aide would not use the same vocabulary in talking to a three-year-old, as she would in talking to the preschool teacher.

How Each Sees the Other

The process of communicating from person-to-person is greatly influenced by the perception that the sender and receiver have of each other. The feelings that a person has toward the other person are reflected in his tone of voice, choice of words, and even in his *body language*. A reference book mentioned in the resource section of this unit, *How to Read a Person Like a Book,* deals with the importance of body language in person-to-person relationships.

The Right Time and Place

Another factor that may be important in interpersonal relationships is the timing of the communication. For example, one of the first things a supervisor should do if he wants to talk over a problem with his subordinate, is ask the question: "Is this the right time and place?" Problems should not generally be discussed in the middle of an office, where other employees, or the public, can hear the discussion. Personal problems should be discussed only in private.

The Effect of Past Experience

In general, the quality of the person-to-person transaction will depend upon the past experience of the individuals. Human beings have acquired most of their opinions, assumptions, and value judgments through their relationships with other people. Past experience not only helps to teach people about effective interpersonal relationships, it is also often responsible for the irrational prejudices that a person displays. A strong bias usually blocks the interpersonal relationship if the subject of the communication concerns that particular bias.

The Effect of Personal Differences

An additional factor in interpersonal communications involves the intelligence and other personal differences of the people communicating. An example of such a personal difference is the *objectivity* of the people involved, as compared with their *subjectivity*. One person may try to be very fair and objective in discussing a point with another person, yet this other person is, at the same time, taking everything personally and being very subjective in his viewpoint. It is almost as if an adult was talking to an angry child.

Such differences can impede the communications flow between two people. In fact, all the factors mentioned in communications should be examined as to whether they block or facilitate interpersonal relationships. *The most effective interpersonal relationships are those that are adult-like in their character.*

4. DEFENSE MECHANISMS IN INTERPERSONAL RELATIONS

Defense mechanisms are attempts to defend the individual from anxiety. They are essentially a reaction to frustration - a self-deception.

Causes for Defense Mechanisms

In order to help understand some of the causes for defense mechanisms, remember the basic human needs:

- *Biological or physiological needs* - hunger, water, rest, etc.
- *Psychological or social needs* - status, security, affection, justice etc.

Fear of failure in any of these basic needs appears to be related to the development of defense mechanisms; attitudes toward failure, in turn, originate out of the fabric of childhood experience. The social and cultural conditions encountered during childhood determine the rewards and controls which fill one's later life. These childhood experiences, and their resultant consequences, affect personality development, the individual's value system, and his definition of acceptable goals.

Individuals who are dominated by the fear of failure may react by using one of these defense mechanisms:

- *Rationalization* - making an impulsive action seem logical.

- *Projection* - assigning one's traits to others.

- *Identification* - assuming someone else's favorite qualities are their own.

Results of Use of Defense Mechanisms

A common factor to all defense mechanisms is their quality of *self-deception*. People cling to their impulses and actions, perhaps disguising them so that they become socially acceptable. Their defense mechanisms can be found in the everyday behavior of most normal people and, of course, have *direct influences* on interpersonal relationships.

A person, for example, who is responsible for a particular job makes a mistake, and the work doesn't get done. When confronted with the problem by his supervisor, the individual puts the blame on someone or something else. This is a very common form of a defense mechanism.

Defense mechanisms can sometimes have *negative influences* on interpersonal communications. They can contribute to the individual forming erroneous opinions about the other person's motives. These mechanisms can alter the perceptions and evaluations made about the individual by other people, Ways to understand these mechanisms must be sought; one solution is to become more aware of the common defense mechanisms, and to become less defensive through greater acceptance of others.

5. THE INFLUENCES OF ROLE-PLAYING IN INTERPERSONAL RELATIONS

Everyone wears a mask and plays a certain role or roles in life. Even if the role one plays is to be himself, that particular form of behavior can still be considered a role. As a public-service employee, one's role is to serve the public. This can be done in a number of ways. Some of the factors involved in public-service roles will be mentioned below:

Exploring Superior-Subordinate Relations

Public-service employees are accountable for their actions. From the entry-level public administrative analysis trainee, to the President of the United States, every public servant must be accountable to either an immediate supervisor, a governing body, or to the public itself. Entry-level public-service employees gain experience and get promoted, but they continue to be subordinates and responsible for their actions, even though they also become supervisors and have people working for them.

Simulation exercises can be developed which will examine the perceptions of the superior by the subordinate. *Authority* and *power* factors may enter in here, as the superior also perceives the subordinate in a particular way. *Dominance* and *need* factors are at work in superior-subordinate relationships, and the style of leadership used *(autocratic, democratic,* or *lassiez-faire)* is a form of leadership role.

Peer relationships can be explored through simulation exercises. The ways in which co-workers perceive each other and the resultant effect on cooperation is one area to be examined. Ways to establish a climate or environment for effective, cooperative relations should be sought.

It is desirable also to simulate, for better comprehension, interpersonal communications with the general public. Role-playing techniques, which permit the exploration of person-to-person relationships, are highlighted in the following section on simulation exercises.

Interpersonal Relations Achieved Through Simulation

The preparation of students for entry-level public-service occupations must include an opportunity to experience meaningful interpersonal relations. Public-service employees, whether office or field workers, experience personal relationships with other people every day. The initial success of the public-service worker will depend in large measure upon his ability to interact effectively with others in the office or field. Accordingly, a principle objective of simulation exercises for entry-level public-service education is to have the student acquire the necessary interpersonal relations skills that make for success in all public-service occupations.

When developing a model public-service simulation with the principal objective being to improve favorable interpersonal relations, certain criteria must be established. These criteria may be stated as follows:

- *Interpersonal relations must be the principal component of the simulation*. Provision must be made for students to interact with others in an office interpersonal setting so that they may work and communicate effectively with one another.

- *The simulation must be as realistic as possible*. Realism can best be accomplished by simulating an actual public-service operation in as many areas as possible.

- *Originality must play an important part*. Model simulations, currently in use, must not be copied in an effort to maintain simplicity.

- *The simulation must be interesting*. Students must be motivated to participate in the simulation and to be enthusiastic about its operation.

- *The simulation must be unstructured*. Provision must be made to allow for an awareness of events as they take place. Students must learn to cope with a situation without prior knowledge that the situation will occur.

In order for the teacher to determine if the model public-service simulation developed has, in fact, improved interpersonal relations, the simulation must be evaluated in terms of meeting the established objectives.

6. ## MEASURING INTERPERSONAL RELATIONS

    ### Survey of Interpersonal Values

    A valid and reliable instrument for measuring interpersonal relations, such as the *Survey of Interpersonal Values,* may be used for this purpose. This instrument is intended for grades 9-12, and is designed to measure the relative importance of the major factored interpersonal value dimensions. These values include both the subject's relations with others and others with himself. The value dimensions considered are:

    - *Support*--being treated with understanding, encouragement, kindness, and consideration.

    - *Conformity*--doing what is socially correct, accepted, and proper.

- *Recognition*--being admired, looked up to, considered important, and attracting favorable notice.

- *Independence*--being able to do what one wants to do, making one's own decisions, doing things in one's own way.

- *Benevolence*--doing things for other people, sharing, and helping.

- *Leadership*--being in charge of others, having authority or power.

A pretest on interpersonal values is administered before the model public-service simulation actually begins, and the same test is administerd as a post-test after a stipulated period of time. By comparison of results, and through the use of applicable statistics, the gain in behavior modification in interpersonal relations can be determined, as a result of using the model public-service simulation.

Analysis of Interpersonal Behavior

Public-service employees should be aware of their own needs, and of the needs of other people. They should be able to recognize situations or behavior calling for professional help, and be able to refer people to such appropriate help. New employees must be able to use their knowledge of person-to-person relationships to effectively work with people.

In order to become more effective in interpersonal relationships, students must gain an understanding of:

- *Self-evaluation* - to be able to assess their own strengths and weaknesses.

- *Group Evaluation* - as a class to be able to evaluate other individuals' competencies in interpersonal communications.

- *Correction of own self-perception* - to be able to do something about the knowledge and attitudes formed by adjusting their individual behavior.

STUDENT LEARNING ACTIVITIES

- Define formal and informal social behavior.

- List the important factors in interpersonal communication.

- View and discuss the film strip, *Your Educational Goals, No. 2: Human Relationships*.

- Role play in alternate supervisor-subordinate relationships practicing effective interpersonal communication.

- Write an essay on "Defense mechanisms affect interpersonal relationships."

- View the film, *The Unanswered Question*, and discuss human relationships afterwards.

- Listen to a discussion of structured interpersonal communications and evaluate the effectiveness of the person-to-person relationship.

- In small groups, discuss the ways in which people are mutually dependent on each other,
- Use simulation exercises to practice interpersonal relations.
- List the different kinds of roles and games played in interpersonal communications.
- Debate the statement: *Understanding person-to-person relations is one of the most important skills a person can acquire for success in life.*
- Discuss how understanding interpersonal relationships can help a person to effectively work with people.
- Define the role of recognizing one's own feelings in relation to others.

TEACHER MANAGEMENT ACTIVITIES

- Have the students define formal and informal social behavior.
- Show transparencies on interpersonal relations, *(Social Sensitivity lour Relationship with Others)* and discuss concepts afterwards.
- Assign written exercises on the important factors in interpersonal communication.
- Set up role-playing exercises on subordinate-supervisor roles in effective interpersonal communication.
- Encourage small-group discussions of the ways people are mutually dependent on each other.
- Show a movie on human relationships *(The Unanswered Question)* and discuss key points afterwards.
- Separate the class into teams to debate such statements as: Understanding interpersonal relations is one of the most important skills a person can acquire for success in life.
- Encourage individual study and reading in interpersonal relationships.
- Assign an essay on the worth and dignity of man in interpersonal relations.
- Bring in public-service workers who deal with others to talk to the class about the value of effective interpersonal communications.

Evaluation Questions

Fill in the crossword puzzle below.

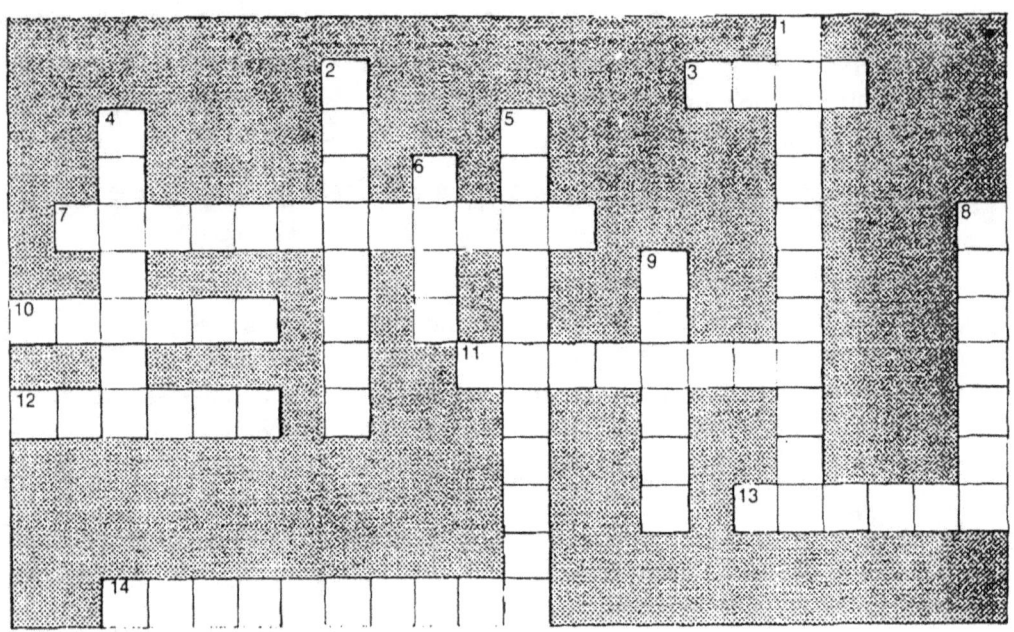

ACROSS:
3. A strong prejudice or _____ can block good relationships.
7. Being able to do what one wants to do satisfies the need for _____.
10. One's _____ of words should be correct for the occasion.
11. Friends usually have an _____ relationship.
12. In talking over problems with others, _____ is important.
13. Everyone needs to feel _____.
14. _____ is assigning one's traits to others.

DOWN:
1. We _____ when we try to make our actions seem logical.
2. When we assume someone's qualities as our own we _____ with that person.
4. Individuals _____ when they do what is socially proper.
5. When we attract favorable attention, we gain _____.
6. Some people have a strong _____ of failure.
8. _____ mechanics help to protect a person from anxiety.
9. A public service worker usually has a _____ relationship with the public.

Answer Key

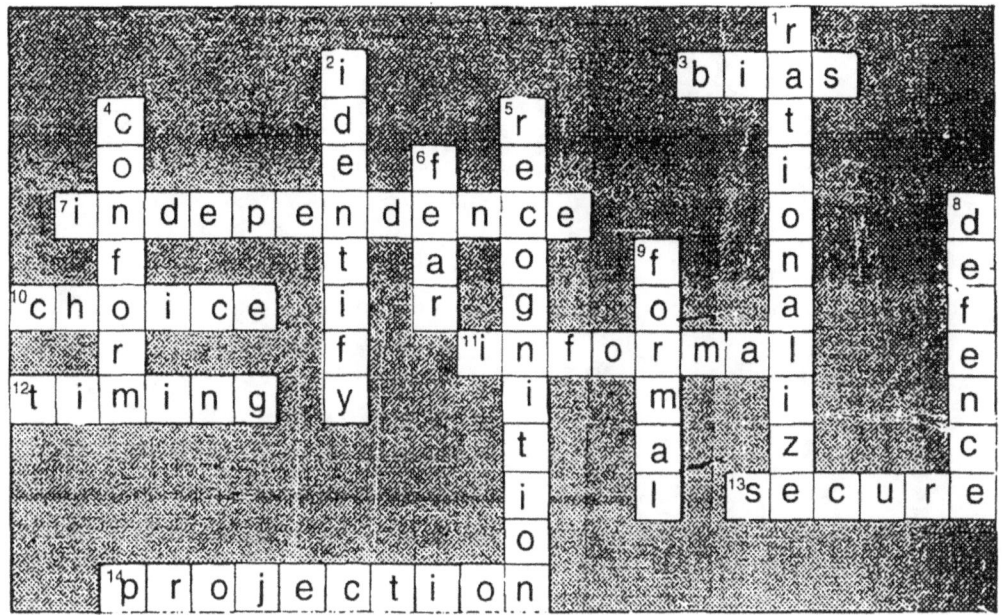

www.ingramcontent.com/pod-product-compliance
Lightning Source LLC
Chambersburg PA
CBHW082206300426
44117CB00016B/2690